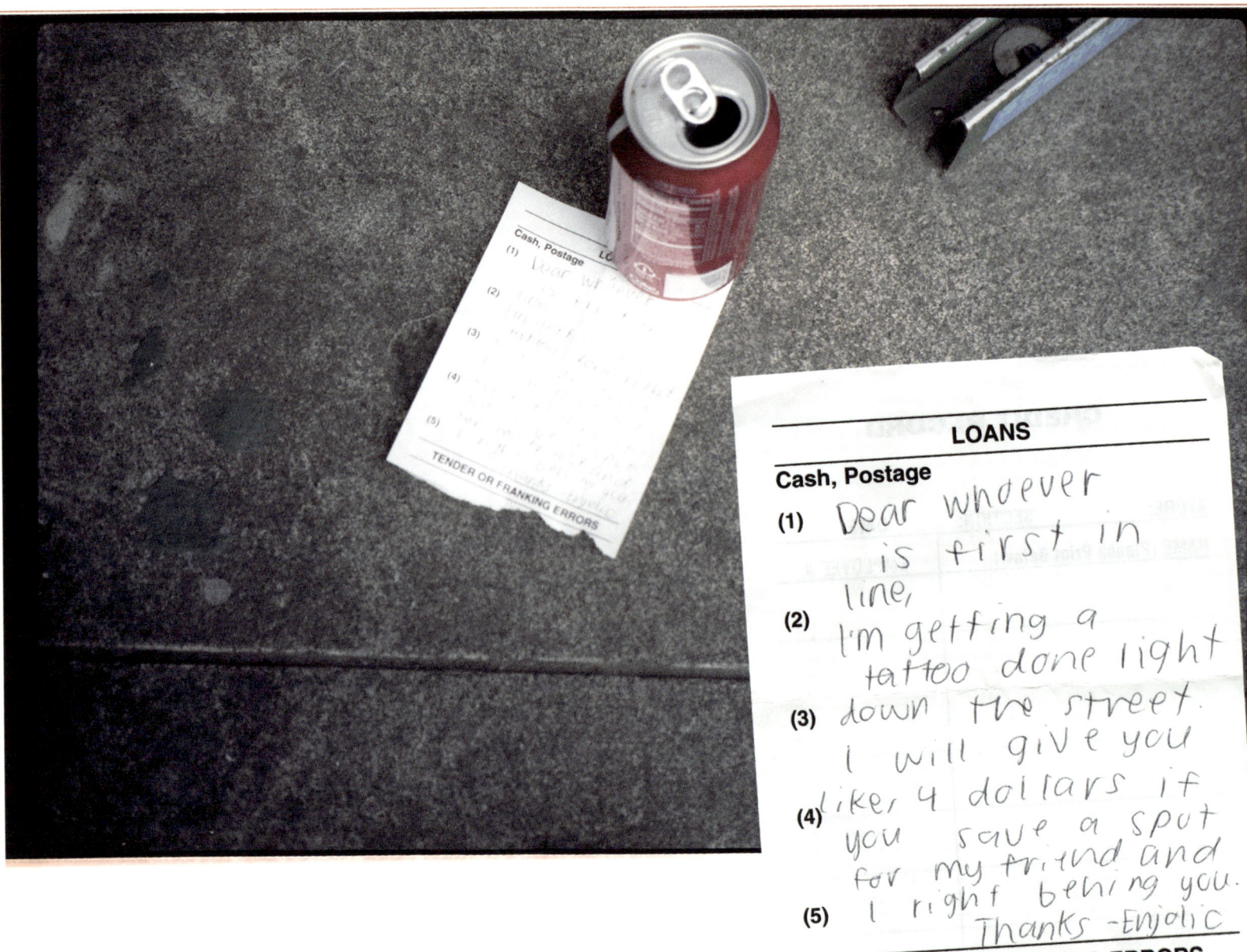

# TABLE OF CONTENTS

Foreword - 4-5

The Making of Suburbia - 6-29

Warped Tour - 30-51

A Whole Year in Airports - 52-75

Pop Punk's Not Dead - 76-99

The Holiday Shows - 100-109

The Glamour Kills Tour - 110-196

Credits - 197-199

# Uh hello?

I never thought this is where I would be. Sitting at home rolling D20's, changing the batteries out of my wavebird controller, getting upset over bent corners on my Hellraiser action figures, and practicing saxaphone (doodlehorn), I never thought I would go on to travel the world for years. Its hard to believe that I have been gigging for seven years now and even harder to believe the last three have been spent with six of my closest comrades... well kind of six except for that bit when there was only five and then six again and well... lets just go ahead and drop that. From Ghostbustour to now, things have changed and this band has grown but everyone in the Crimson Lover (our van) has stayed the same, well except for that fact that everyone's hair has gotten shorter and shorter over the years. We have done countless tours now, riding in different sized vehicles, with sometimes just myself and sometimes multiple friends, and the one thing I've always noticed is how these dudes tackle each situation the same. Everyone is still just a guy, doing guy things. The same punk ethics from years ago are present in their daily lives. We have been to almost every state playing all kinds of rooms from house shows to larger theaters, traveled to over a dozen countries, shared the stage with so many talented musicians, all the while maintaining the same level heads and hungry stomachs. Especially Nick with the hunger. So many creepy gas station snacks. Its incredible to still see Dan come out and speak with kids post gig. Sometimes bands get burnt out but these guys just keep pushing. I've truly been told by so many human beings how this band's music/lyrics have helped them out of rough spots in their lives and that has to be one of the biggest accomplishments a band could ever have. Matt will take the time to answer any questions, concerns, and thoughts via the world wide web and people don't forget that. Its comforting to be spoken to as another human being rather than a fan and the guys keep it real. Friends all over the world love these guys for who they are and what they represent. A unit that has come from nothing with no help from anyone and continued to thrive and grow the right way, the true way, the respectable way, by putting in the effort, love, and care to create something that so many can relate to. Heck, Josh recently received shirts with his name printed on the inside of them. Just shows you how much sticking with something since day one can pay off. Genuine music performed by genuine people.

Here we are June 12th, 2012 broken down in Senora, Texas with a defunct alternator just reminiscing about touring then and now. Michael using his book light attached to his shirt (looking like a flamboyant alien) to flag down a truck to help with a jump. The intoxicated man telling us of his women escapades as he then speeds off swerving down the highway. Making it 10 miles down the road to find out that every hotel is booked for the evening. Taking a long stroll to a gas station to ask someone for help with another jump while making a pit stop at a DQ scaring all 4 sheltered employees. Finding 3 weary Californian travelers to help us out in exchange for filling their gas tank. Driving 30 miles to an Economy Inn to find that the owner feels bad for us so he throws in an extra room with no A/C for free. Waking up to bugs on our faces to bring the Crimson Lover to Victor's auto shop. Coming to pick up the rejuvenated El Diabla to find a man with a walker working underneath an automobile. And finally back on the road to San Antonio to keep the gig alive. Sometimes things like this happen and we handled the situation the same way we would have years ago. No complaints, just action, and seeing that really solidified for me how honest these vagabonds really are. The fact that we are able to get up and seize the day despite any hurdles or obstacles brings a strong feeling of relief and faith. Faith is what pulls it all together, and faith is what these guys have had in each other from day one. As I've learned from becoming close with family and friends, they have all had that fireball of dedication inside of them since birth. It's a safe feeling knowing you have a second or third or fourth family out there. To be able to go to Casey's place and feel welcomed like a brother and second son from mom. Its what keeps the machine afloat.

Here in front of you is a collection of thoughts, images, and feelings that I can best describe as seeing how the last few years have been through our eyes. A scrapbook of hard work that has brought these men to where they are at now. As we finish up watching RAW in the van I can officially say how excited I am for you to browse through the events of our past year of life. Similar to the story of an underdog being pushed around in the ring, it has been one of my greatest adventures watching this team grow and move on to become the champion it is today. Built from the ground up off of nothing but stale beer and sweat, it has finally flowered into a remarkable display of talent and perseverance that has truly paid off. I'm glad I'm in their corner ready to be tagged in to take on any kind of challenge/opponent. This stable isn't going anywhere but the top, and it's going there in the most sincere and honest way. From front to back, this book will prove that to you. See you on the other side.

"If God built me a ladder to heaven, I would climb it and elbow drop the world."  -  Mick Foley


We built this city on Rock N' Roll.

Namaste

-John James Ryan Jr. (Dad)

Clockwise from top left: Valley of Fire State Park, Red Rock Valley, Hoover Dam and Bonnie Springs Ranch in Red Rock Valley of Howard Hughes fame.

Las Vegas

PRINTED IN USA

7 87109 06079 0

PC4-043 6079

Hey Brother,

Hope all is well back east. Never forget we're always here for you, even if the rest of the world isn't

Love, TWY

To: Hank the Pigeon

Lansdale, PA

Published & Distributed by: Donmar Gifts & Souve... 225 South Valley View Blvd.
Las Vegas, Nevada 8911...

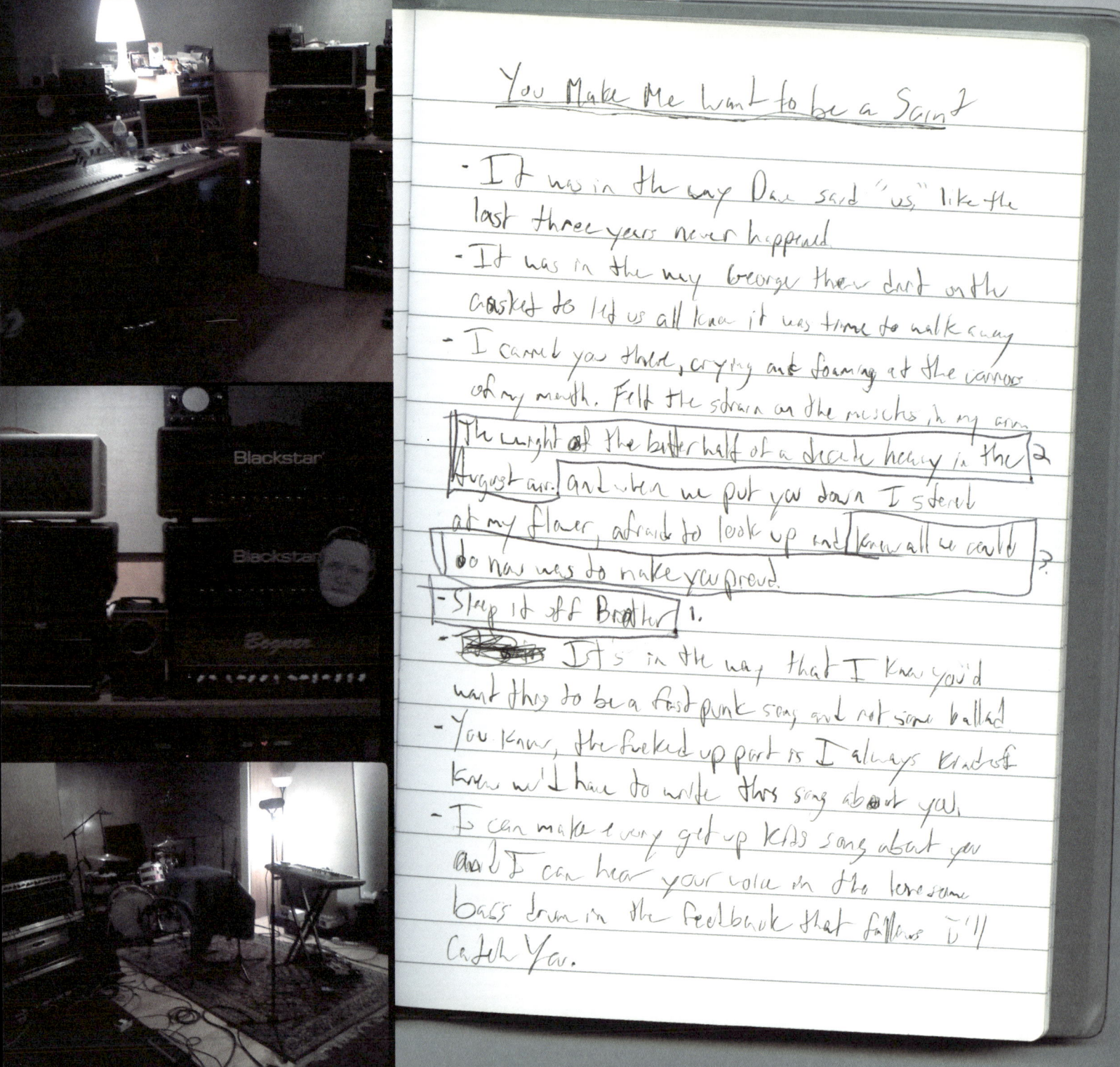

## You Make Me Want to be a Saint

- It was in the way Dave said "us," like the last three years never happened.
- It was in the way George threw dirt on the casket to let us all know it was time to walk away.
- I carried you there, crying and foaming at the corners of my mouth. Felt the strain on the muscles in my arms. The weight of the bitter half of a decade heavy in the August air. And when we put you down I stared at my floor, afraid to look up and know all we could do now was to make you proud.
- Sleep it off Brother.
- It's in the way that I know you'd want this to be a fast punk song and not some ballad.
- You know, the fucked up part is I always kind of knew we'd have to write this song about you.
- I can make every get up kids song about you and I can hear your voice in the lonesome bass drum in the feedback that follows. I'll catch you.

## woke up older

This time when I stacked a Duk novel on a Black Isbll record, what it looked like was what it was. You said you were running late to meet your sisters and I appreciate that you kissed me goodbye. Caught myself in the mirror when I carried a box out of what was our room and I aged ten years last night. [When John introduced woke up new in St. Augustine I knew I wasn't alone]*

Called up Max when I thought I broke my hand punching the drawer. What a way to start off the year. I used to pretend that I didn't like your voice but I'd ~~[scribbled out]~~

*When I woke up here without you, there was nothing to do but collect myself and go home.
[I'm carrying two years worth of memories in the bags under my eyes and watched you leave ~~back out of~~ the room ~~as~~ receding^ in my hair line]

I've been avoiding Rittenhouse like the plague. I don't think I could handle bumping into you today.

## Sunbury

The bowling alley burnt down. They said it was a cigarette and I almost believed it. There were burns in the carpet but everyone knows it was for the insurance.
Other than Hall & Oates the most famous guy from this town played leatherface.
The bus stops by the YMCA next door where I had grown up down the street from Morgan's Mom's shop where I got my suit for prom. Everything else on this street died a long time ago.

Don't Let Me Unfold / Collapse / Cave In

You drove me all the way up here cuse you could tell that I was a mess I wasn't gonna make it to dinner and I shouldn't be calling again. You drove me all the way up here then asked if we could stay in bed because you got work early tomorrow and don't mind if I'm sleeping in

I remember watching them take down the Sears Tower as a kid and the clip plays in my head while I'm getting Mexican food with Evan in Logan Square Chicago. I keep thinking of my bones doing the same thing

There were two boards used in the making of Suburbia. One was mostly to satisfy my anxiety. I think the other was mostly to satisfy Steve's and to give us something to look forward to.

In Late November and December, when writing the record, we bought a white board and subdivided it into 13 pieces to represent the 13 sets of lyrics I had written for the record. The goal was to write music to the lyrics so that the mood would fit the words in the same way that someone writing music for a movie would watch the scene he or she was writing for before composing. The white board allowed us to see the progression of the record as each square not only told us the key, tempo and feel of each song but how far along we were. Every day after practice we would rate the songs on a 1 to 10 completion scale. We'd add the scores up and divide by the possible 130 points to find out exactly what percentage of the record was written.

January rolled around and we headed west to record the album with Steve Evetts. We spent 3 days in pre-production and 19 days in the studio tracking. Steve said it was the fastest he's done a record since "Shorter, Faster, Louder" but that was all the time we had. In fact, if we had stayed in the studio another 15 minutes, we'd have missed our flights to Ireland for the Kerrang Tour. Never-the-less, the most important thing to us and to Steve was that the record sound natural and honest and he beat the shit out of us (lovingly) to make that possible. Kennedy lost 4 pounds tracking drums. I threw up twice in the vocal booth from pushing so hard. Everyone lost sleep and sanity but after you finished a track, Steve had a jar of markers waiting. He had made a giant poster with all of the songs and all of us listed on it. When you finished a song, you drew in your box. It kept us organized and light-hearted and clinging above the abyss of total psychosis.

-DC

The guy on the radio sounds like a budget Stephen Hawking and keeps trying to tell me that the bible says the world's ~~gonna~~ ending ~~this~~ goes down around May 20th so I guess this song is pointless. No one's ever gonna hear it. But if the world ends I hope I'm in my living room with good friends

We don't have trouble sleeping. No one is gonna take that away from me
I'm going to bed tonight in my New Found Glory hoodie
Fuck the world and what it wants me to be

This week is gonna swallow me but when it spits me out the other side I'm landing on my feet

Fuck some movie I was convinced Keanu Reeves was in. It's fear mongering shit that Modern Day Mayans don't even believe in

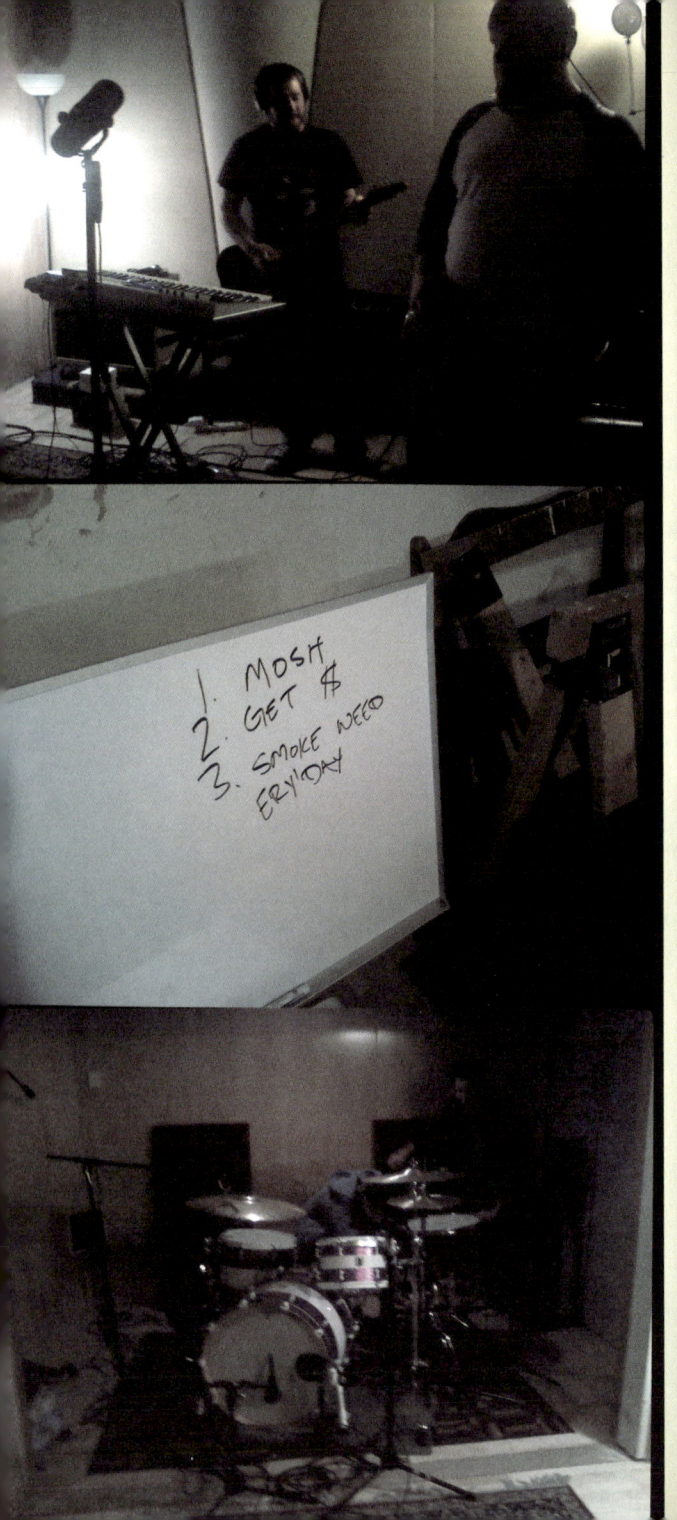

# My Life as Kob Gordon

Kelly says that at the end of each relationship, boys start quoting lyrics from that movielife song. My mom say there's no songs with her name in them except one about a crackhead and Janie's got a gun. Max says after I mentioned him in bar bands, kids started asking questions. It got weird kind of quick. I had a dream that we named a kid we never had after Hannah Hold on and I haven't listened since. It tears me to pieces. Someone keeps ~~putting~~ on all of the sad songs. I keep singing along. The jukebox turns and I'm gone. I ~~blew~~ pumpin' ~~of~~ all my quarters ~~dying~~ lookins for ~~to find~~ the perfect swan song to leave on. Stevie said that when I woke up feeling helpless, I should think about it different. That I had it all wrong. It's not the end if you call it a new beginning plus it's a chance to write some fucking bitter songs I heard Kristen belt the note to some words that Alex wrote about dying alone and I felt kinda whole. It takes a fucked up head to think about dying alone when you're in your 20s so I'm glad it's not just me. It takes a fucked up mind to think about dying alone so I'm glad it's not just me.

The graffiti over 309 used to say things that I could romanticize like "I'll always love you Katie" or "Bernard Herman lives" or maybe "loves." I could never quite decipher or decide. Now the overpass says things like "Drat" and I don't know what to make of it.

I'll Always love you Katie...

The highway looks enticing
I keep thinking about where I would go and who I would leave behind.
Of course I've found a way to be nostalgic about a year that I hated and if we stayed 18 forever I'd have offed my self already. The Brand New joke wont be necessary
I remeber me at 19, ~~laying~~ naked in your parents basement ~~hazy eyed and~~ young and careless watching you blow smoke rings.

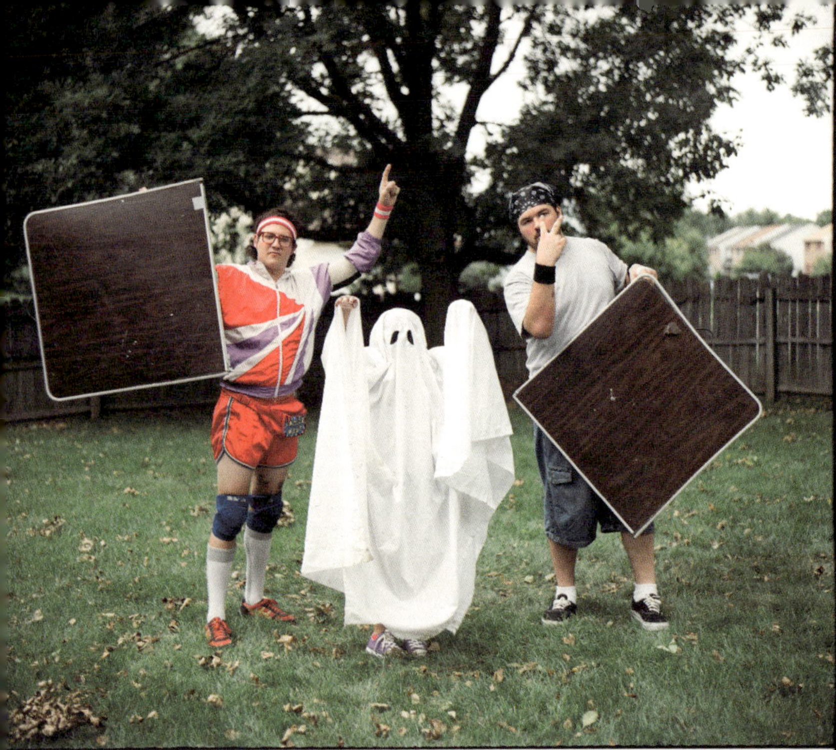

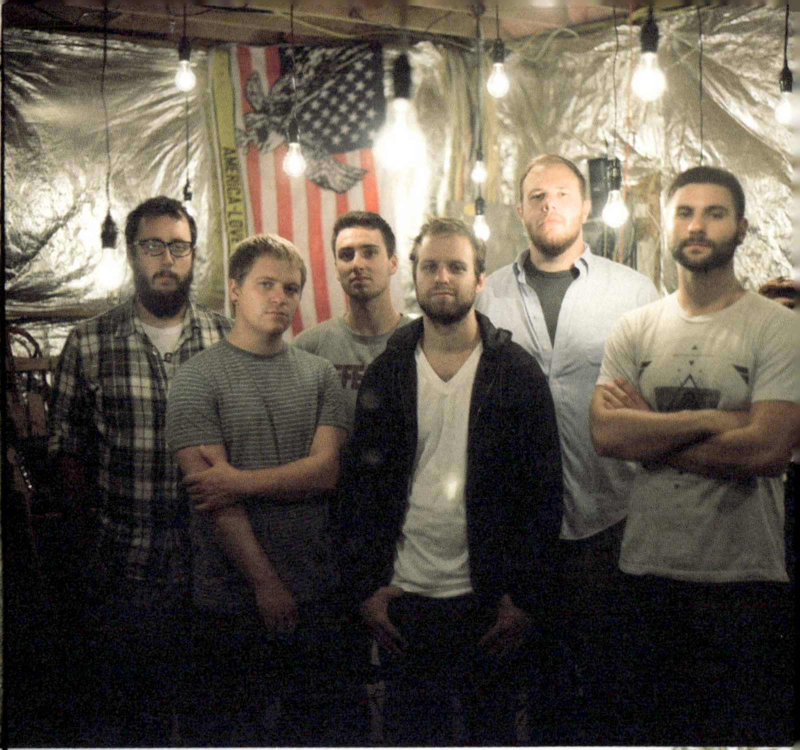

It was cold and grey all day but the Hank suit kept me pretty warm. It was a long day and when we were shooting the cover @p on the roof I actually fell asleep in the suit. So, I mean, I might be asleep in the picture on the cover of the record. —AM

this is me staring out the window the morning of our suburbia release show. That was a crazy day for all of us. I guess this is the calm before the storm

—JM

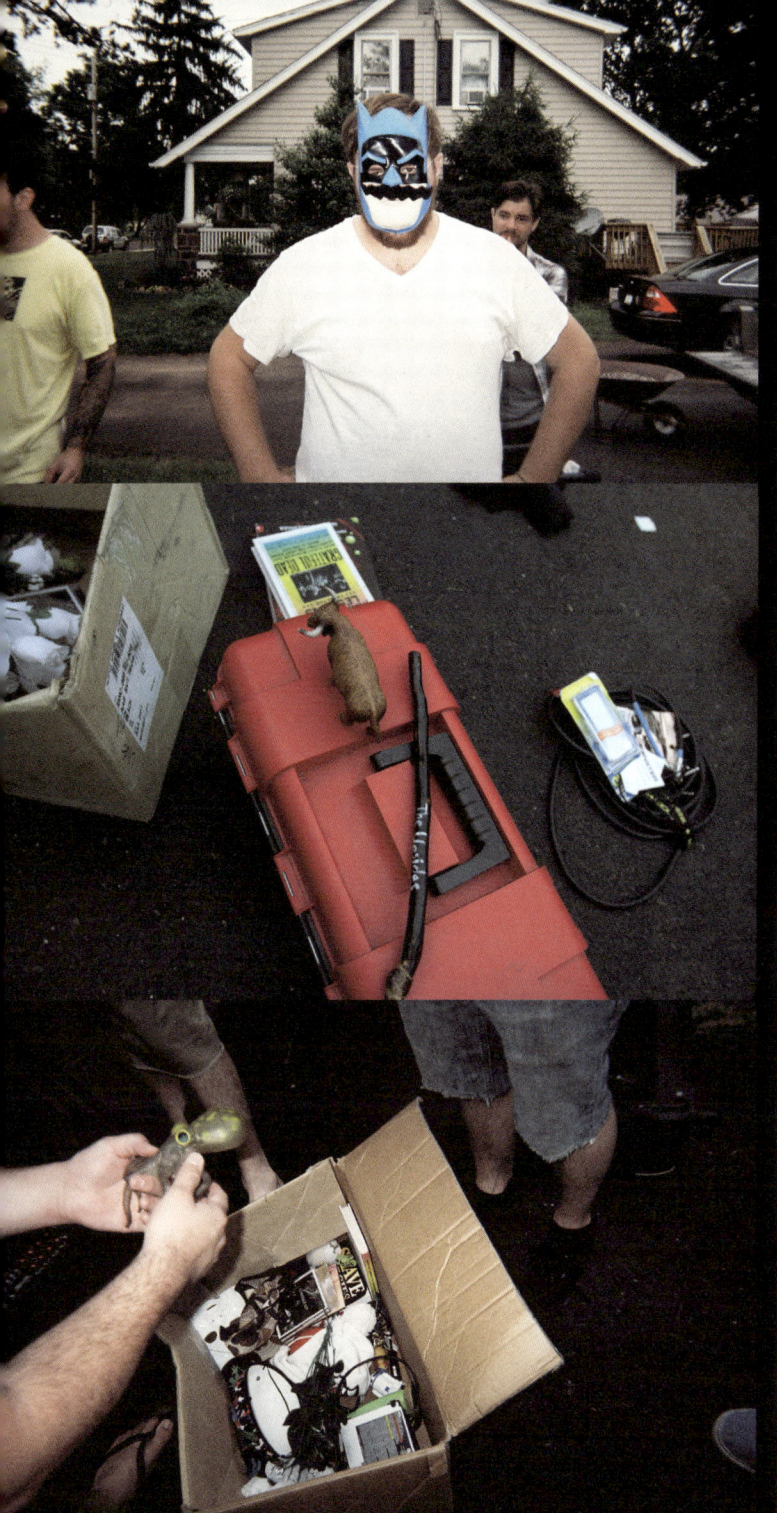

So, throughout our tenure as a band, we've assembled an army of weird shit. Some things we bought, like the plastic toy bull with realistically sized testicles (to scale of course). Others were given to us like the batman mask that a pair of dudes bought us instead of their bus ticket home or the magic wand. At least, we think it's a magic wand. Some guy gave it to us after a set in NE PA. The venue was rushing everyone out the door so he couldn't explain it. It came with a note but it was just a rap about ear-orgasms. Anyway, we have a ton of things like this and we kept them all on the dash of the van to dick around with on long drives and to use for photoshoots but while we were cleaning the van out to drive to Arizona to start warped tour, we had to take them out. So, we boxed them all up and now they hang out at our house.

-DC

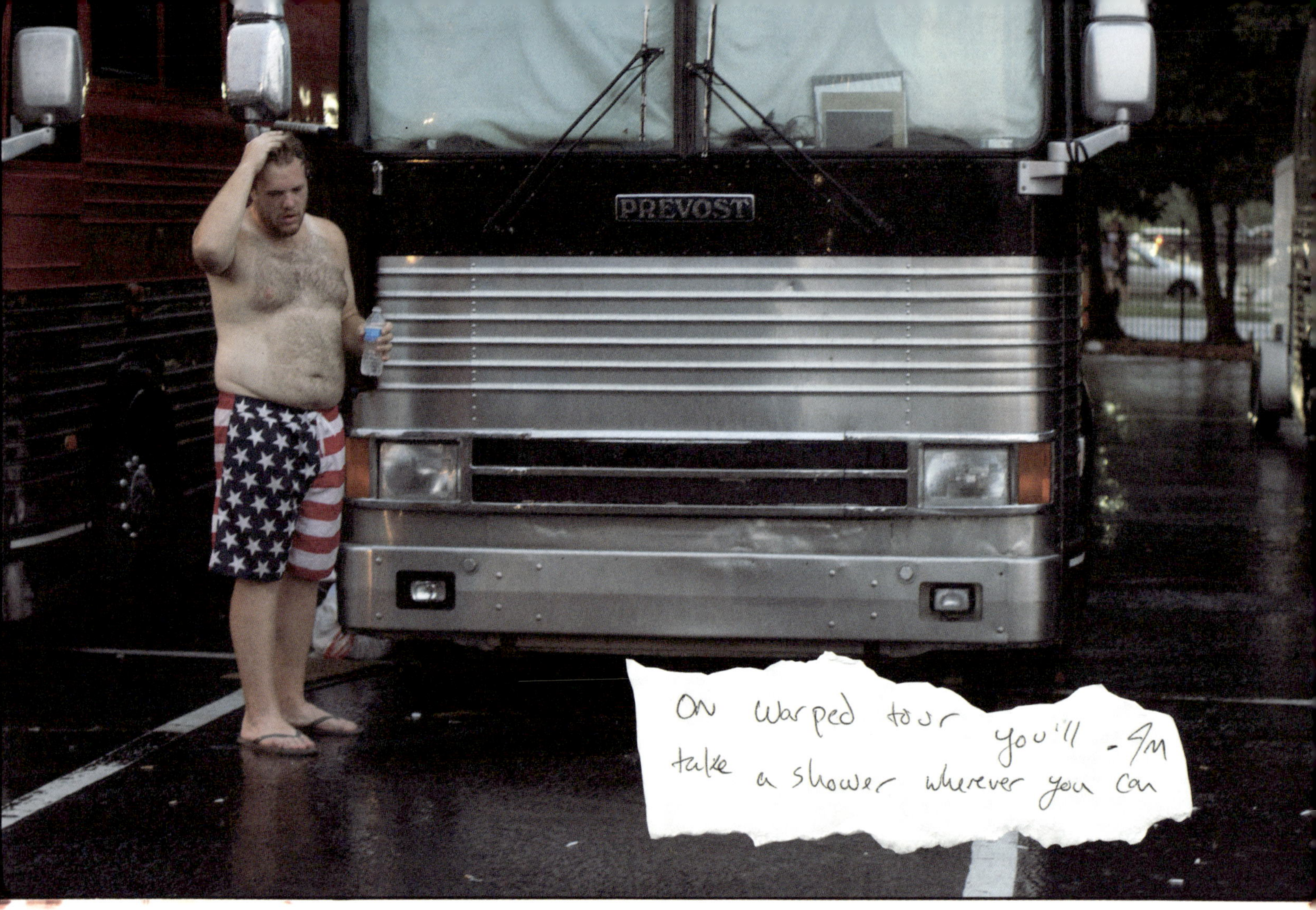
PREVOST
On warped tour you'll take a shower wherever you can -JM

HOPELESS RECORDS

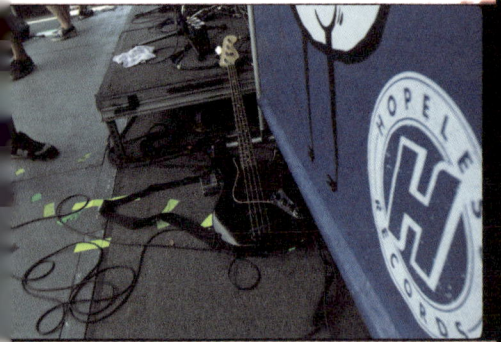

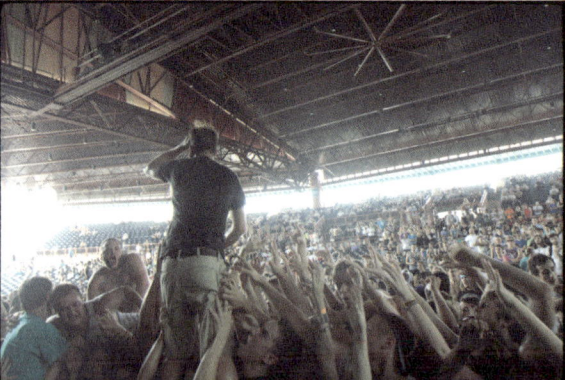

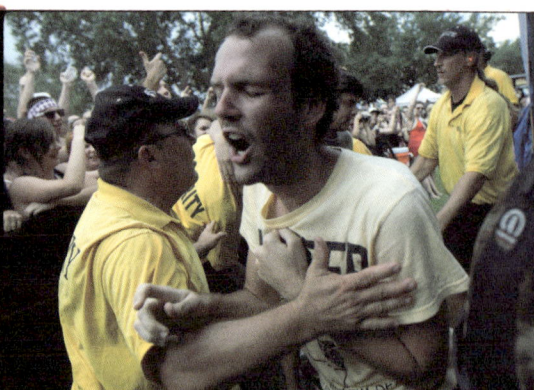

SUPERVISOR

the WONDER YEARS
ETHOS
I'M SO BORED
I'M NOT BORED ANYMORE

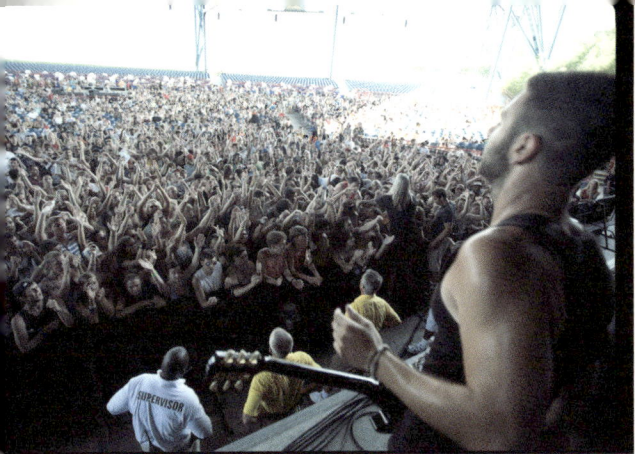

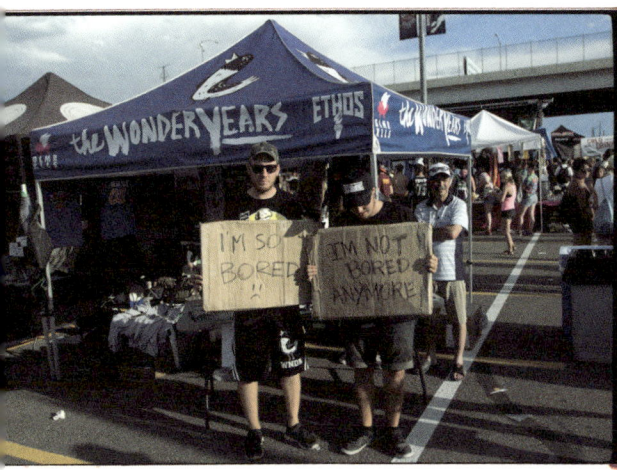

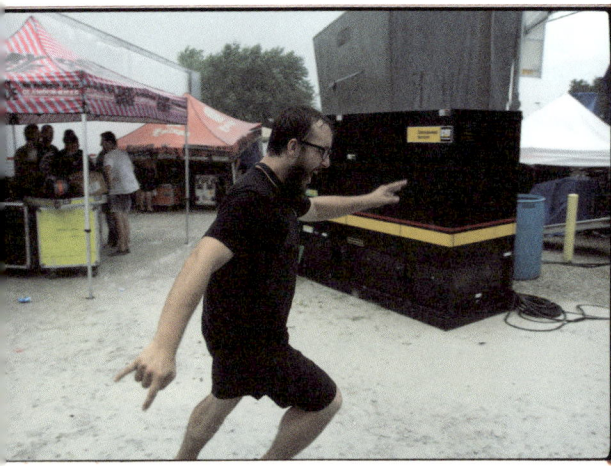

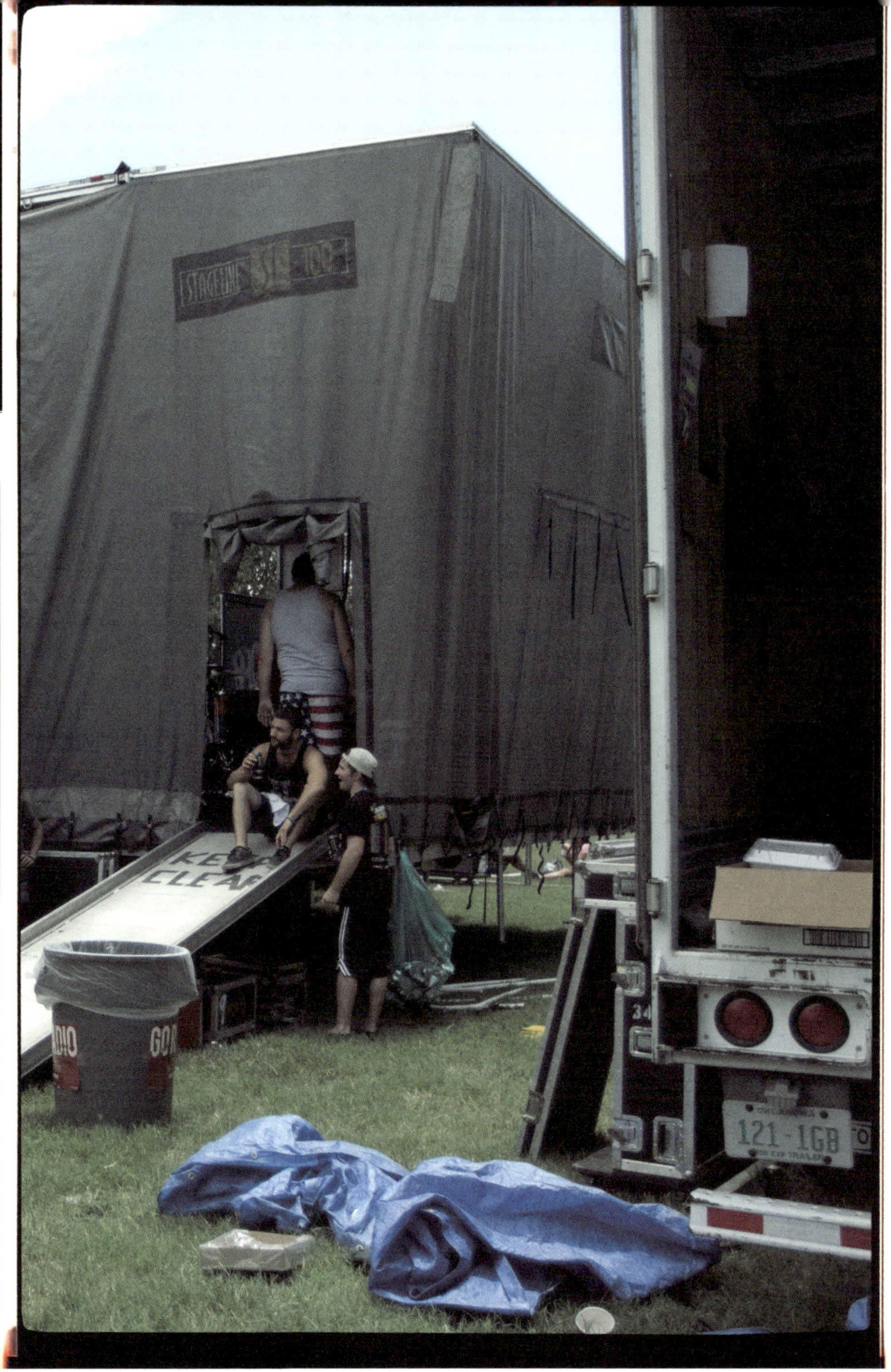
STAGELINE SL 100
KEEP CLEAR
121-1GB

When I realized my 24th birthday was going to be spent in good ol' Idaho I was not especially pumped. However, thanks to awesome friends, poor decisions, and the kindness of Idahoan horse breeders, it went down as one of the best.
        -MDK

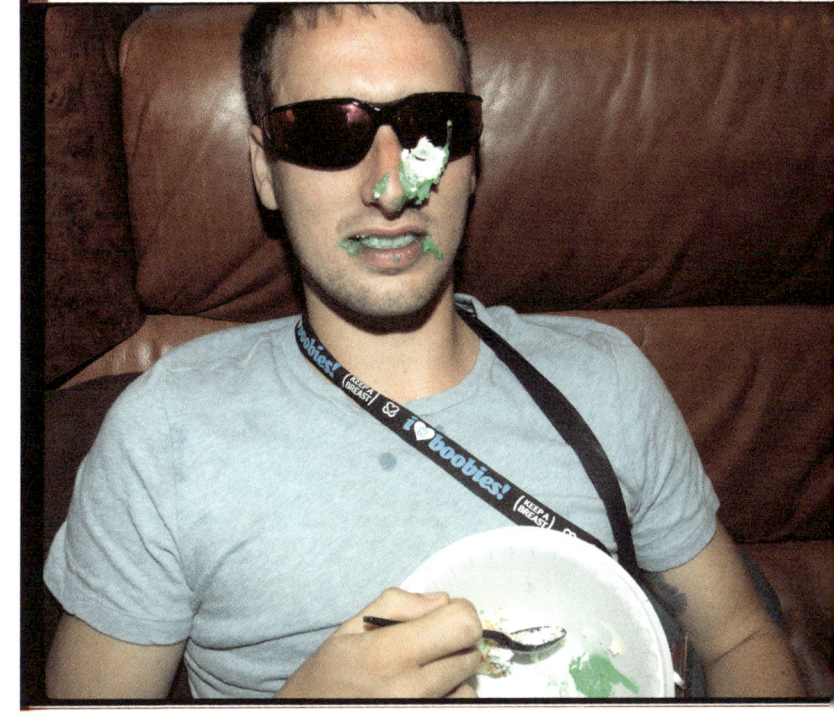

Rules of Wizard Staff
1. DRINK BEER
2. TAPE EMPTIES TOGETHER
3. WHEN STAFF IS TALLER THAN YOU, YOU HAVE ACHIEVED WIZARD STATUS
4. I GUESS SOUPY CAN DRINK SODA INSTEAD

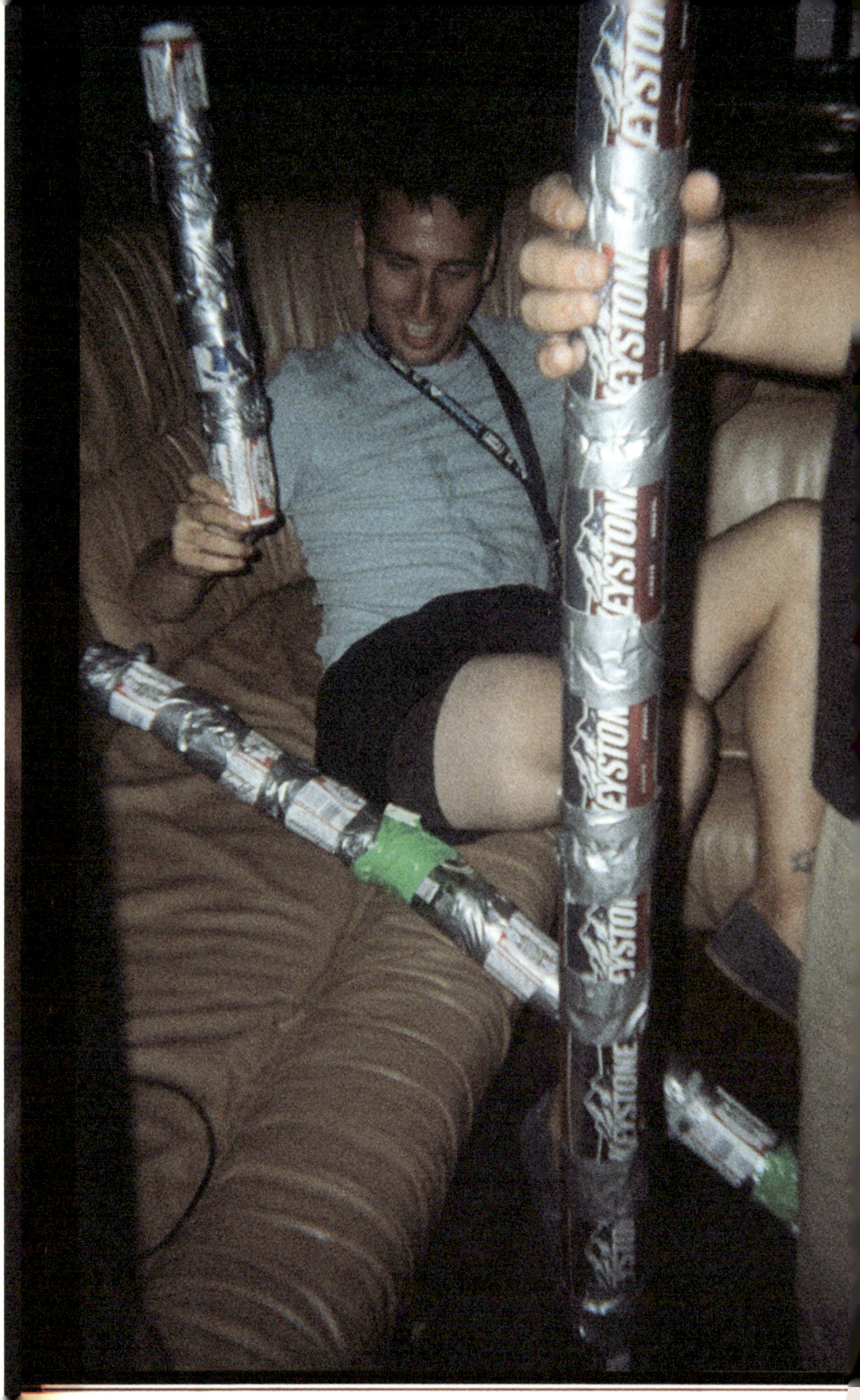

With the help of Jenny D, I was able to take my supreme facial hair growing ability and bring home yet another championship for #ourteam. We officially won Warped Tour.

- ML

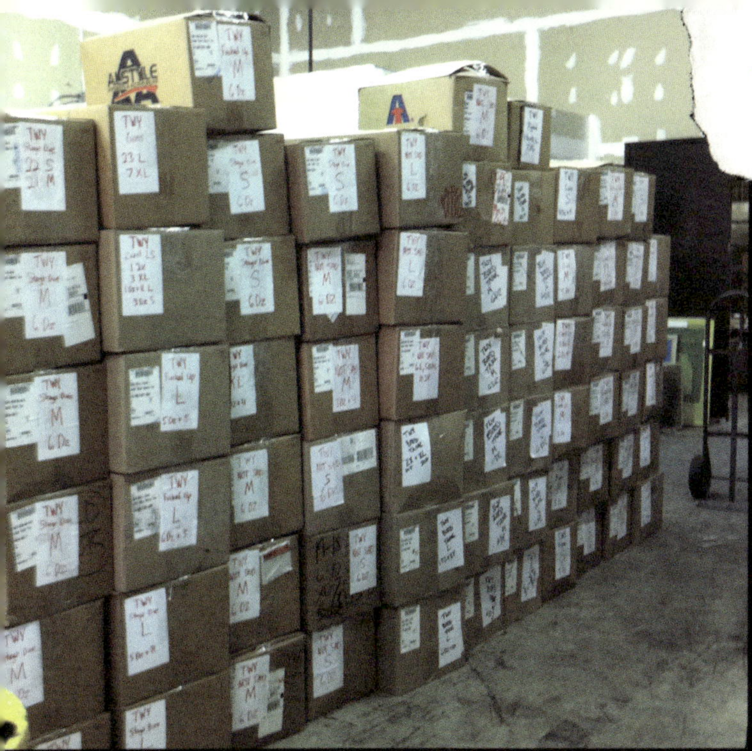

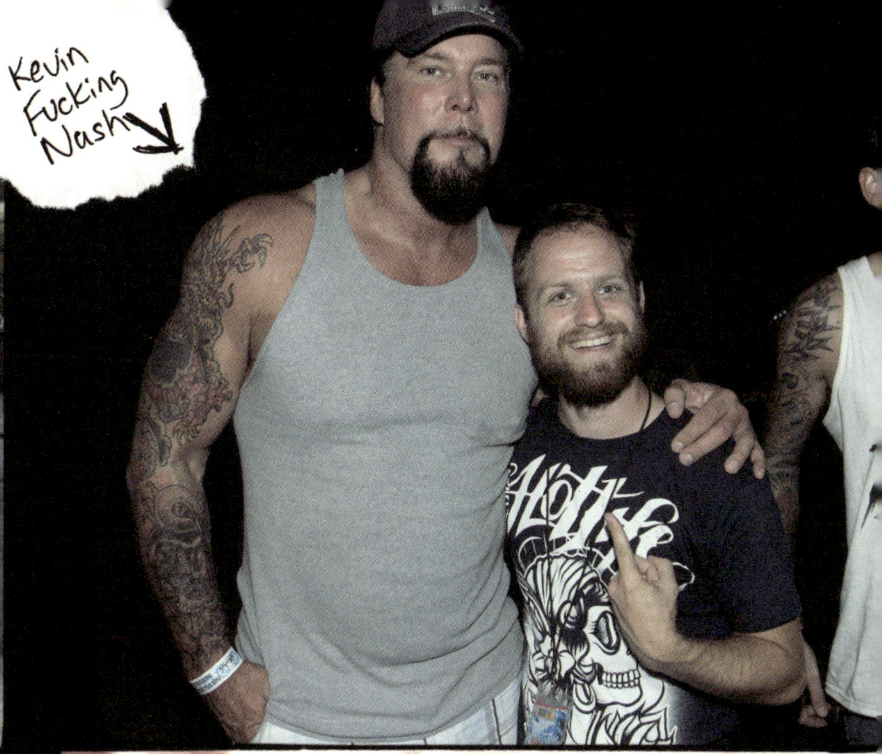
Kevin
Fucking
Nash

TIP ME
MY DAD FINGERS
ME

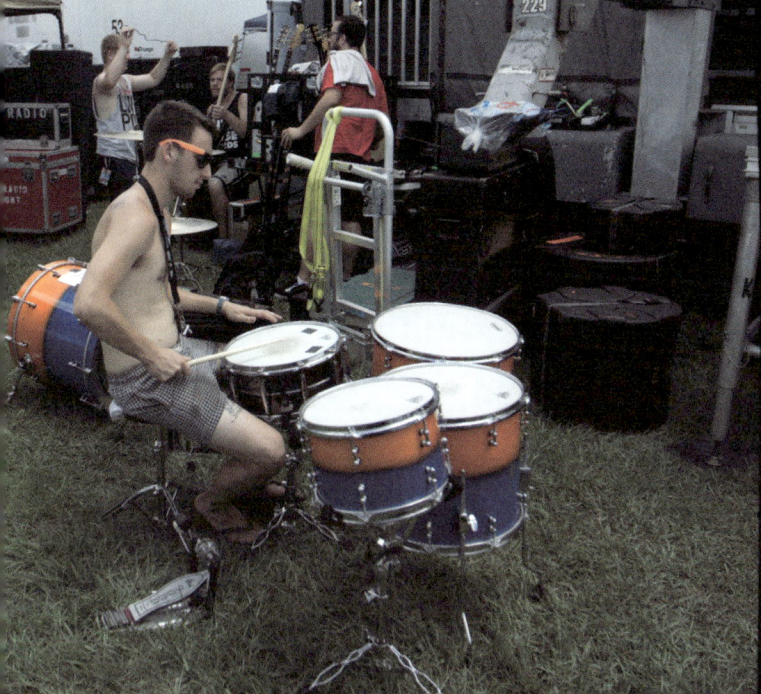

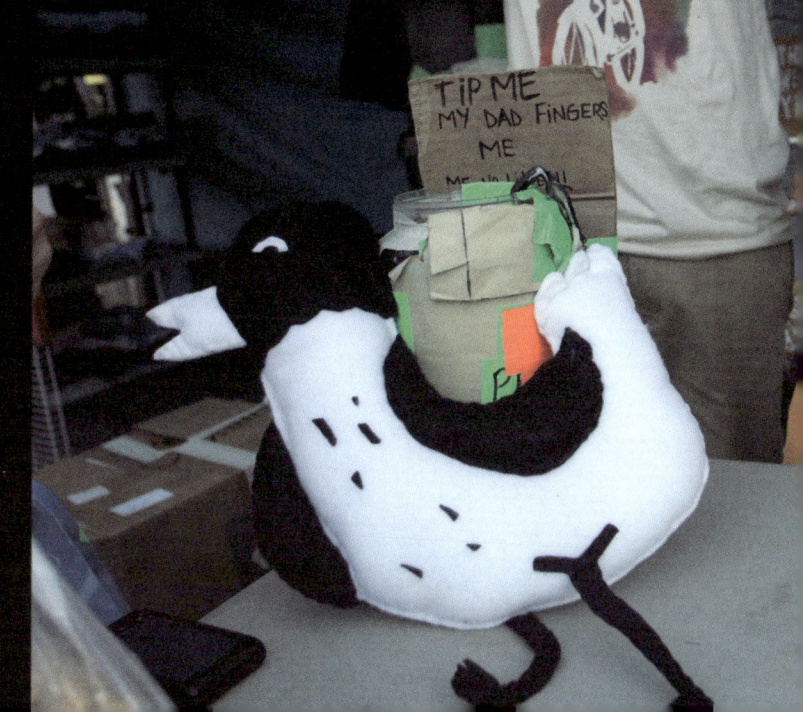

In Europe bands aren't allowed to leave your van running so if you're stopped you have to plug the van in. This leads to parking the van next to an available power source which is always terribly placed. One day we had to park in the middle of a college campus on the first day of classes

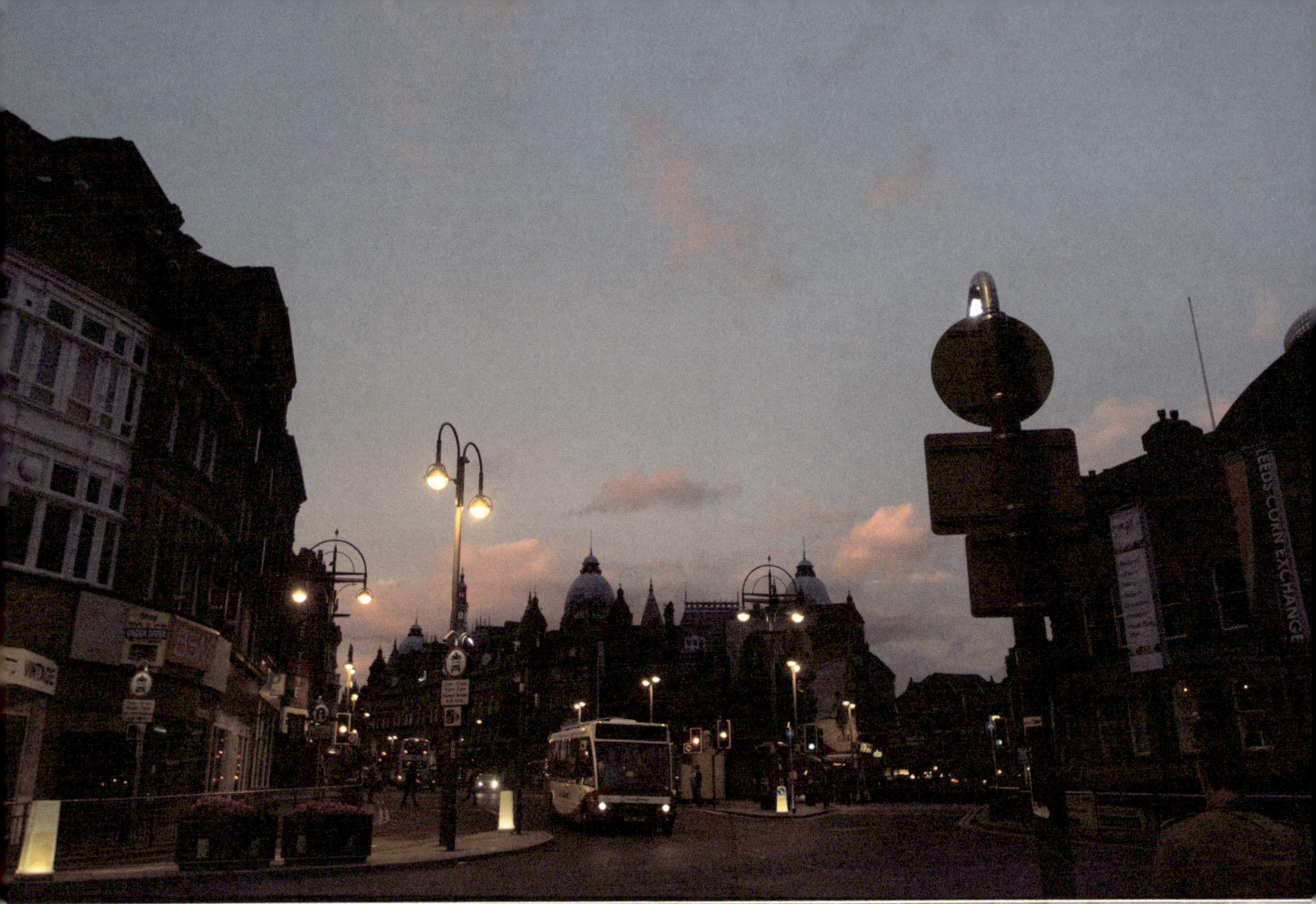
LEEDS CORN EXCHANGE

HALAL FOODS
PIZZAS
BURGERS
KEBABS
FRIED CHICKEN
OPEN

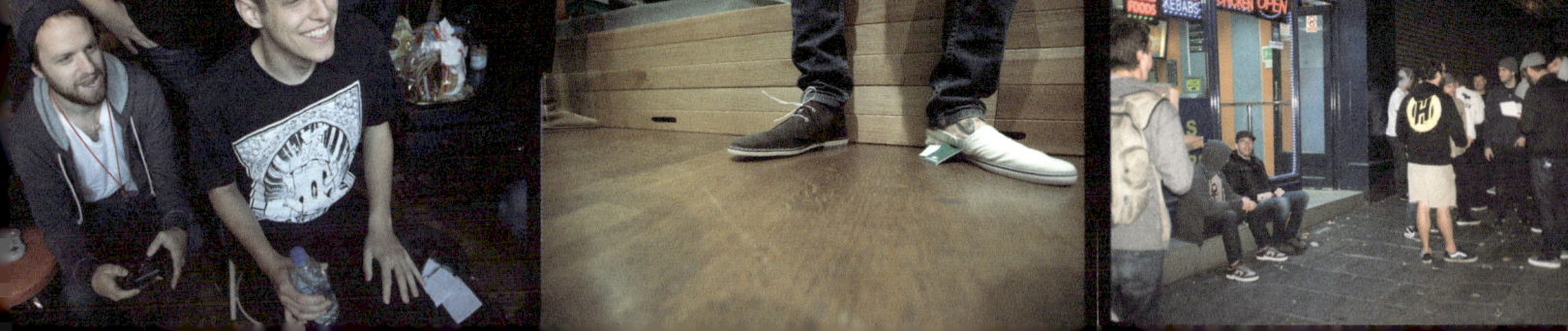

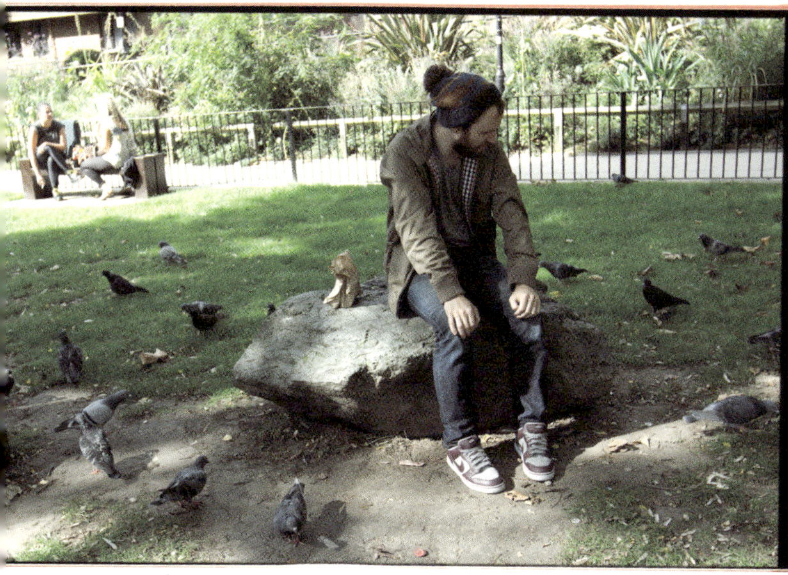

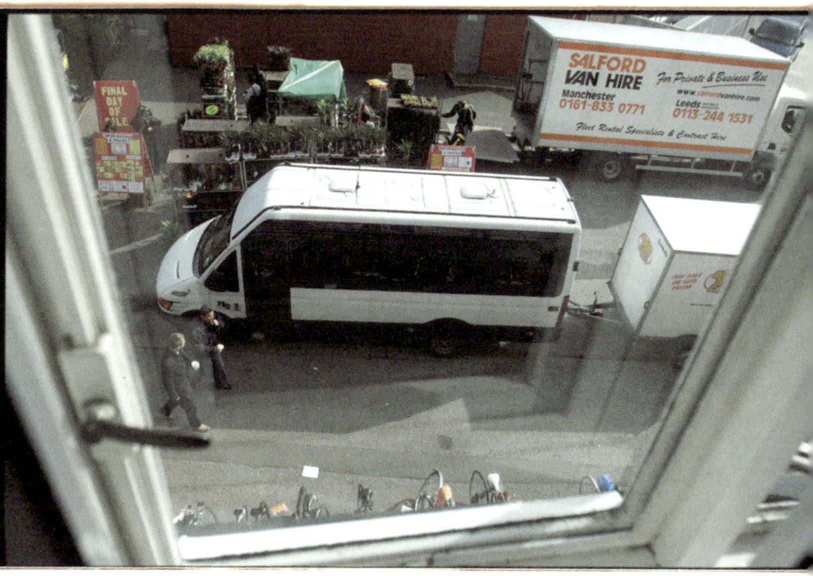
SALFORD
VAN HIRE
For Private & Business Use
Manchester
0161-833 0771
Leeds
0113-244 1531
Fleet Rental Specialists & Contract Hire

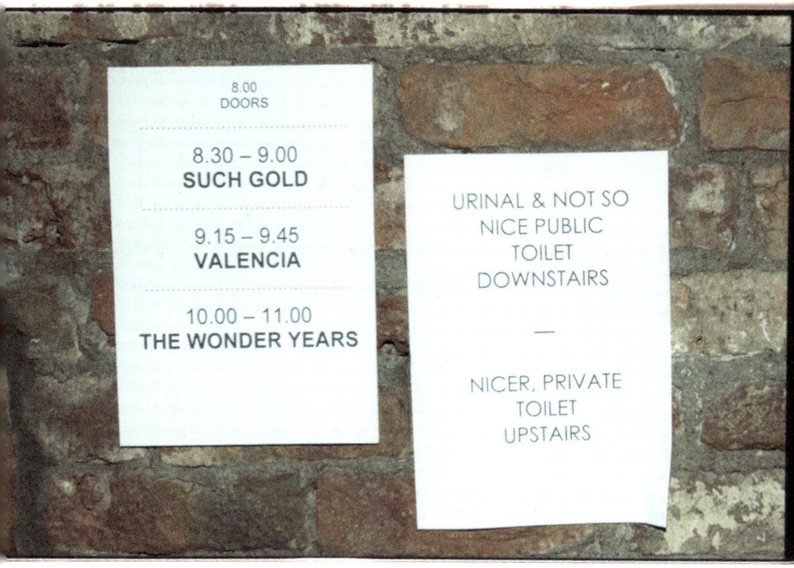
8.00
DOORS
8.30 – 9.00
SUCH GOLD
9.15 – 9.45
VALENCIA
10.00 – 11.00
THE WONDER YEARS
URINAL & NOT SO
NICE PUBLIC
TOILET
DOWNSTAIRS
—
NICER, PRIVATE
TOILET
UPSTAIRS

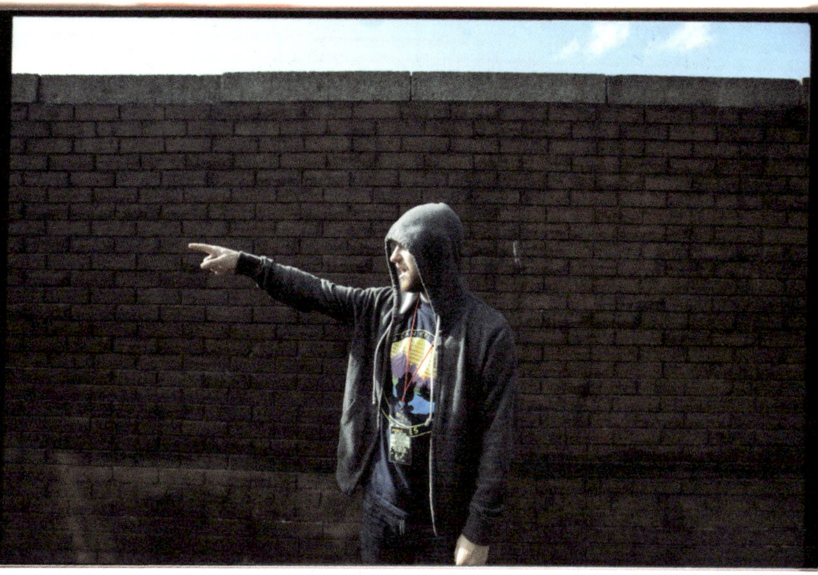

I'm not much of a club guy but there is some kind of weird appeal to punk discos in England. More often than not I found myself getting drunk at these on the A Whole Year in Airports tour with Valencia and Such Gold. -MB

Crowd surfing to the bar and back.

I'm fairly uncomfortable around drunk people. Mostly the loud, obnoxious ones. My "friends" left me with this woman who was screaming incoherently at the staff in this small kebab shop while I waited for my food. She eventually puked on the floor and we all saw her underoos. I think she ~~~~ ordered almost everything on the menu. —NS

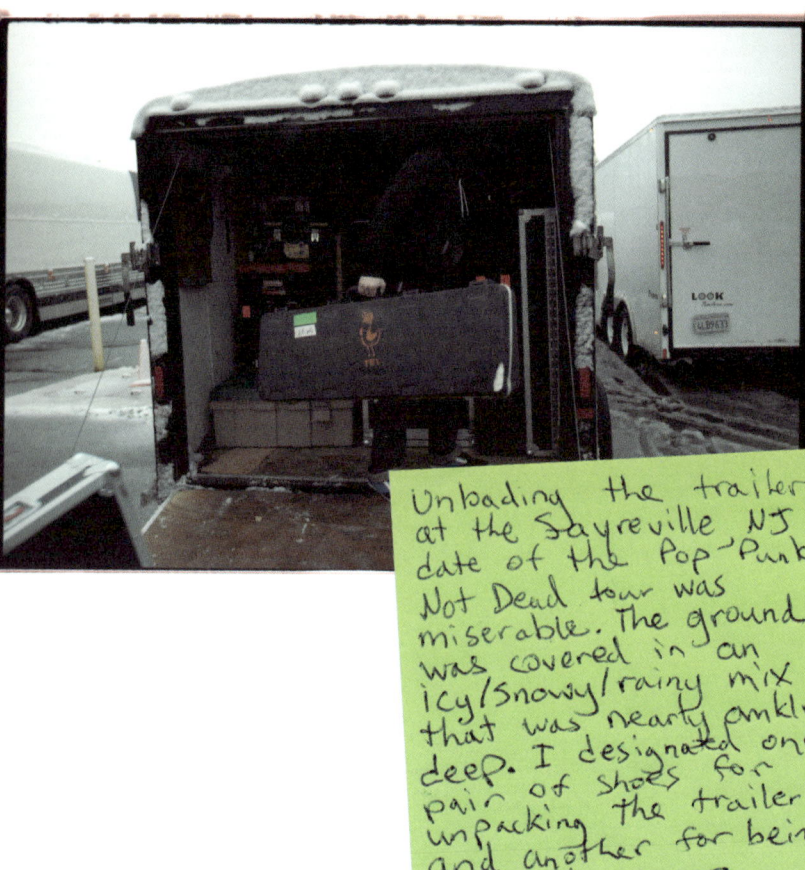

Unloading the trailer at the Sayreville NJ date of the Pop-Punk's Not Dead tour was miserable. The ground was covered in an icy/snowy/rainy mix that was nearly ankle deep. I designated one pair of shoes for unpacking the trailer and another for being inside the venue. The hand dryer in the men's bathroom doubled as a shoe dryer that day.

—MB

```
              MELT BAR AND GRILLED
               6700 ROCKSIDE RD

  Server: Melody
  Table 31/3                            11/01/20
  Guests: 5                              2:37
                                          201

  DIET PEPSI
  FRIED TOFU                              2.
  KINDERGARTEN                            5.
     SUB VEGAN CHEDDAR                   15.
     ADD TOMATOES
     ADD GRILLED ONIONS
     ADD GREEN PEPPER
     ADD MUSHROOMS
     ADD AVOCADO
     ADD TOFU
     ADD DEEP FRY

  Subtotal
  Tax                                    22.
                                          1.
  Total
                                         23.

  Balance Due                           23.7

     Thank you for dining with us.
```

Things to do on a long van ride.

1. Sleep.   2. Read.   3. Watch the world burn.

—DC

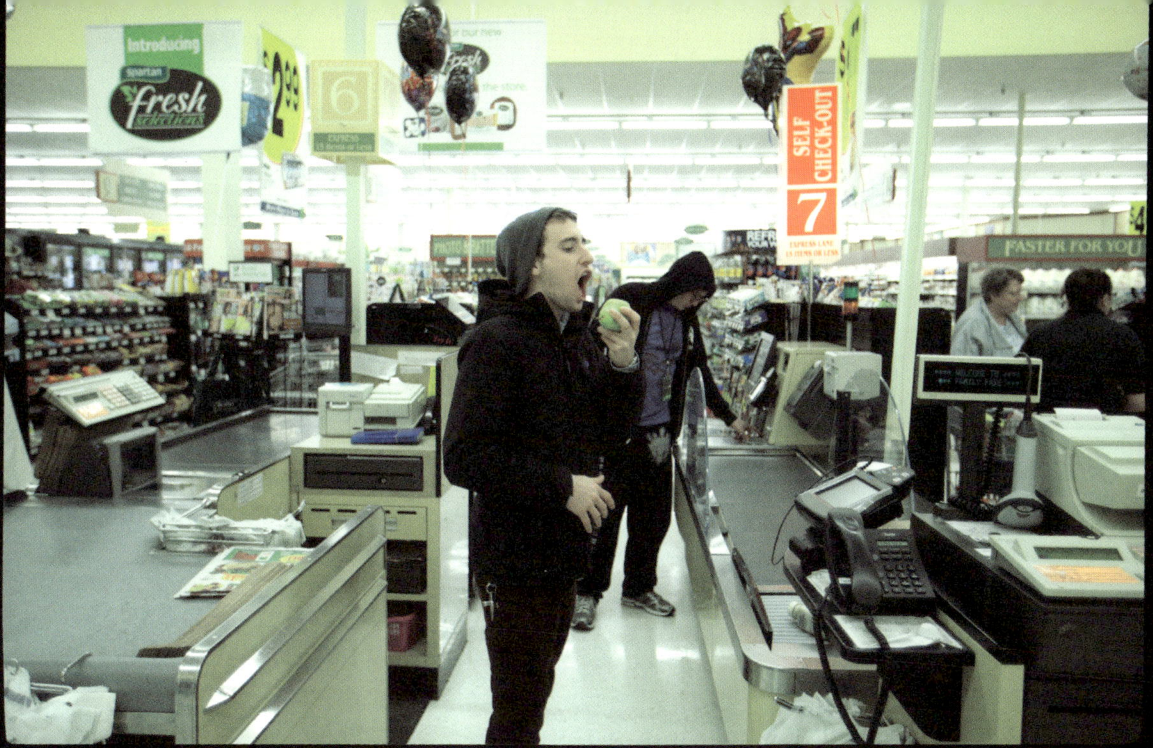
Introducing
spartan
fresh selections
SELF CHECK-OUT
7
FASTER FOR YOU

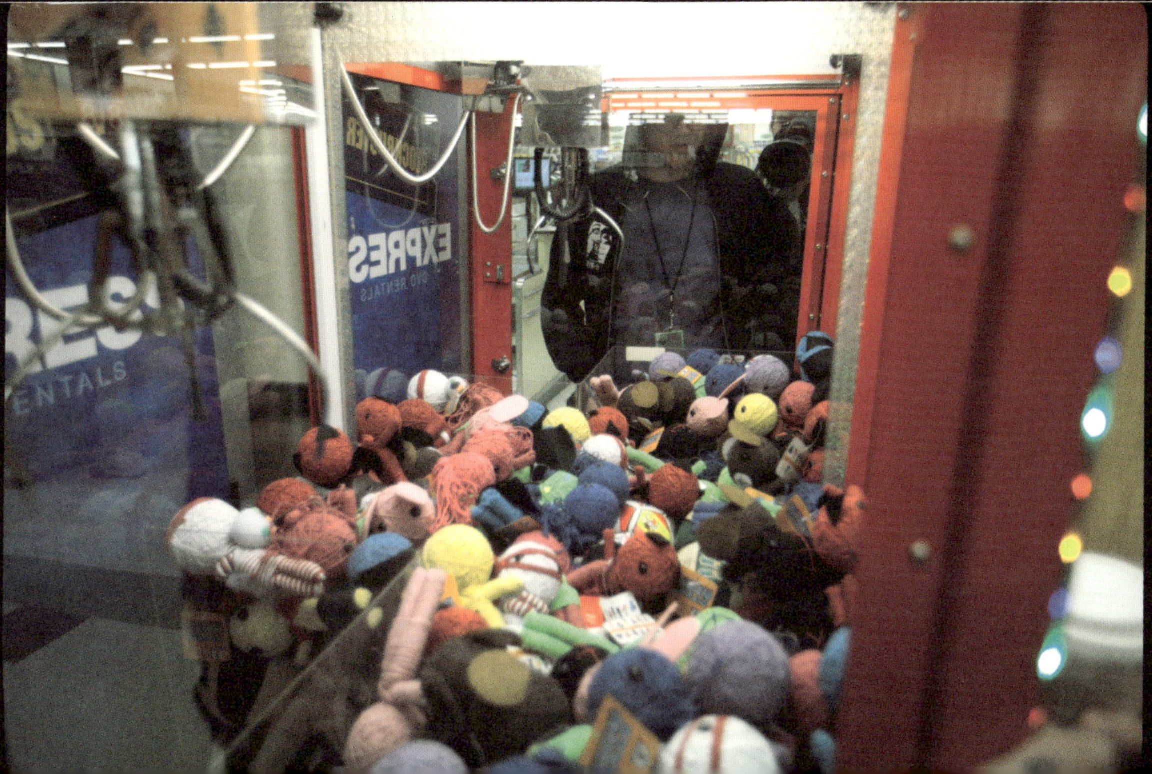

R5 PRODUCTIONS PRESENTS:

# THE WONDER YEARS
## THE LOST TAPE COLLECTIVE HOLIDAY SHOW

MAN OVERBOARD
FIREWORKS • WHEATUS

INTO IT. OVER IT
MOVING MOUNTAINS
12/16/11 • UNION TRANSFER

This horrid woman tried kicking us out of this hotel. She didn't know what rapport meant. -DC →

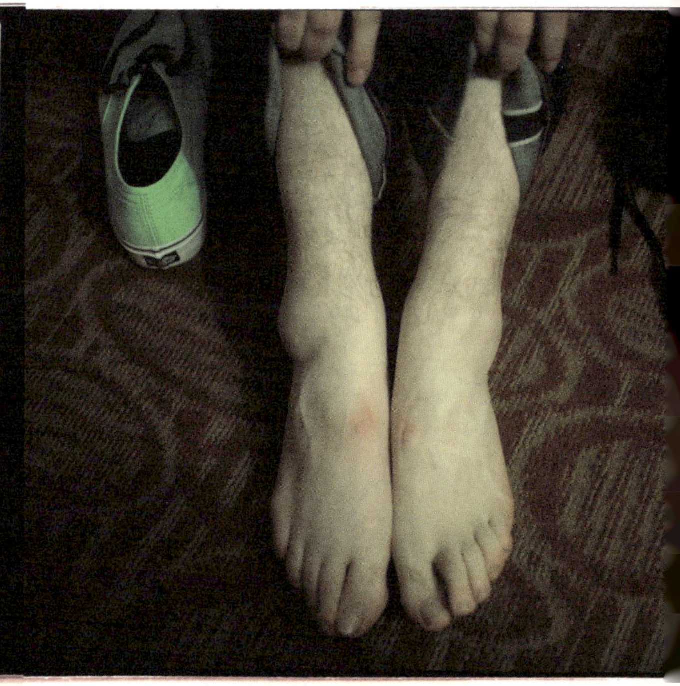

# BREAKFAST

**AMERICA'S PLACE TO WORK, AMERICA'S PLACE TO EAT.**

## Try one of our many SPECIALTY WAFFLES

| | Price | Calories |
|---|---|---|
| WAFFLE (Single/Double) | 2.95 & 3.94 | 380-760 |
| Pecan WAFFLE | 3.45 | 540 |
| WAFFLE with | | |
| Sausage or Bacon | 5.30 | 500-700 |
| City Ham | 5.50 | 470 |
| 2 Eggs* (any style) | 6.20 | 890 |

### Try one of our Waffle Toppings
CHOCOLATE CHIPS, PEANUT BUTTER, BLUEBERRY or STRAWBERRY ...... .25 ea. ...... +95-160

## EGGS*
Served with Toast, Jelly and Grits
Substitute: TEXAS Biscuit for Toast +150 cal, Hashbrowns for Grits +25 cal, Tomatoes for Grits -165 cal

| | Price | Calories |
|---|---|---|
| 3 Eggs | 3.65 | 580 |
| 2 Eggs | 3.25 | 510 |
| Cheese 'N Eggs | | |
| Served with Raisin Toast & Apple Butter | 4.05 | 680 |

**WH 300** Egg whites only ("Hold the Yolks") .add .50 ...... -55/Egg

## TODDLE HOUSE® OMELETS*
Served with Toast, Jelly and Grits
Substitute: TEXAS Biscuit for Toast +150 cal, Hashbrowns for Grits +25 cal, Tomatoes for Grits -165 cal
Make it a 3-Egg Omelet for only .40 more +70 calories

| | Price | Calories |
|---|---|---|
| Ham & Cheese | 5.25 | 890 |
| Fiesta | 5.80 | 925 |
| Ham, Cheese, Onions, Tomatoes and Jalapeño Peppers | | |
| Cheesesteak | 5.90 | 1070 |
| Cheese | 4.00 | 820 |

**WH 300** Egg whites only ("Hold the Yolks") ...... .50 ...... -55/Egg

## STEAK* & EGGS*
Served with Toast, Jelly and Hashbrowns
Substitute: TEXAS Biscuit for Toast +150 cal, Grits for Hashbrowns -25 cal, Tomatoes for Hashbrowns -190 cal

| | Price | Calories |
|---|---|---|
| RIBEYE & Eggs, 8 oz. | 9.75 | 1260 |
| T-BONE & Eggs, 10 oz. | 9.75 | 920 |
| STEAK & Eggs, 5 oz. | 7.95 | 830 |
| COUNTRY HAM & Eggs | 6.60 | 800 |

## EGG* SANDWICHES, TEXAS BISCUITS & MELTS
Texas Melts served on Texas Toast with DOUBLE Cheese

THE 3rd ANNUAL

# GLMR KLLS

## TOUR

FEATURING

### THE WONDER YEARS
### POLAR BEAR CLUB
### TRANSIT

The Story So Far    A Loss For Words

INTO IT. OVER IT.

## ALL ACCESS

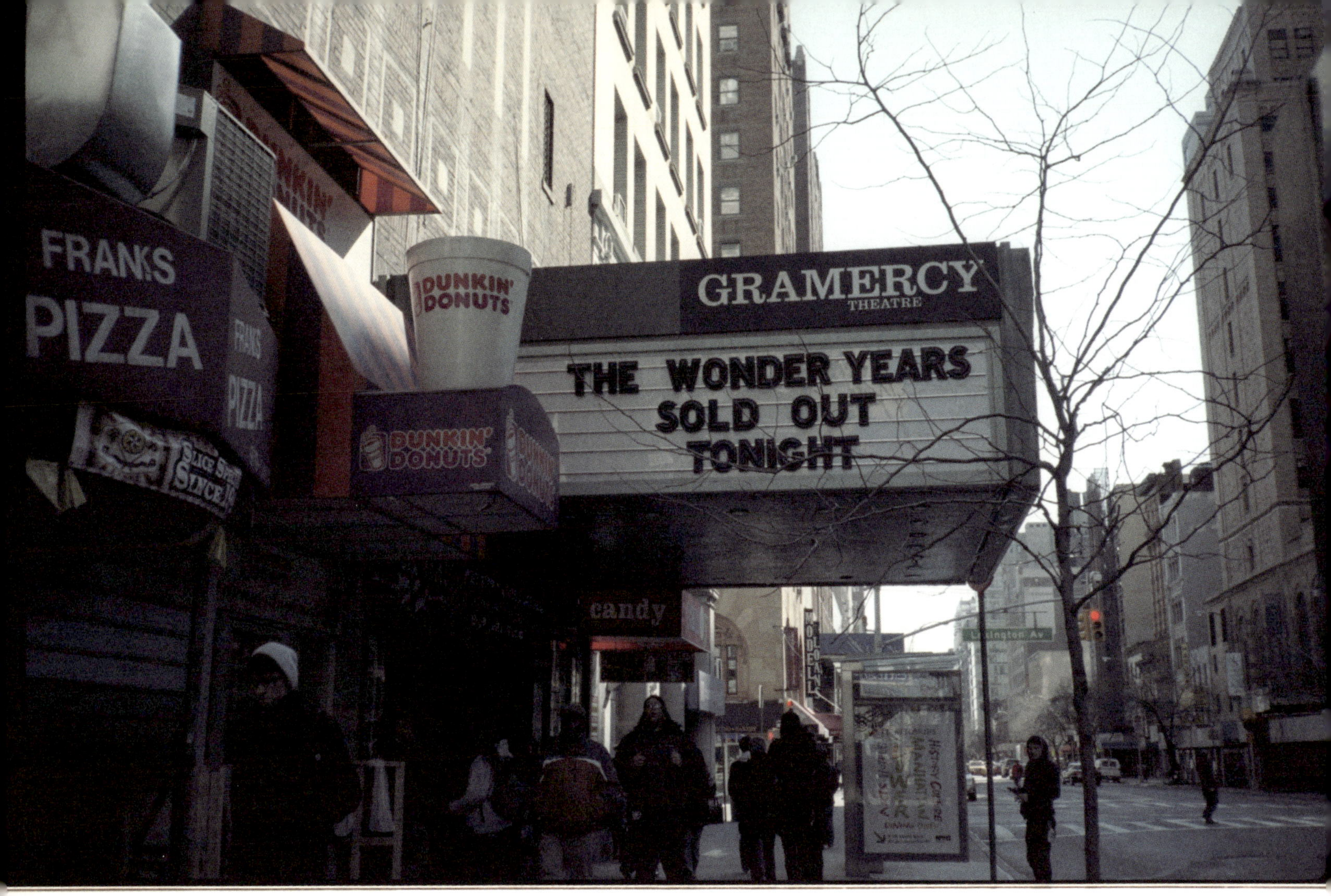
FRANKS
PIZZA
DUNKIN' DONUTS
GRAMERCY
THEATRE
THE WONDER YEARS
SOLD OUT
TONIGHT
candy
Lexington Av

THE TIRED

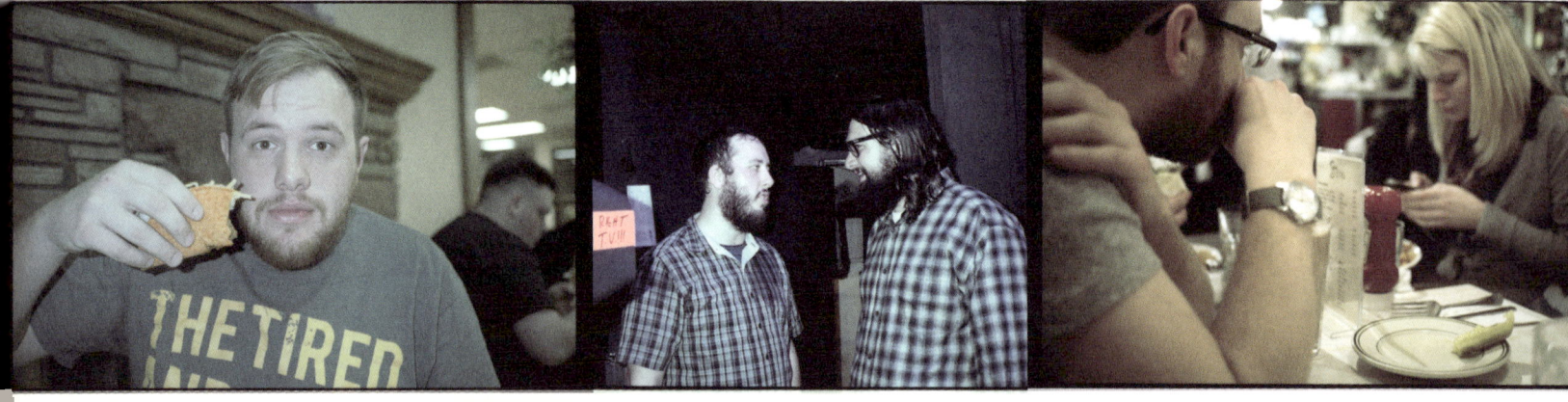

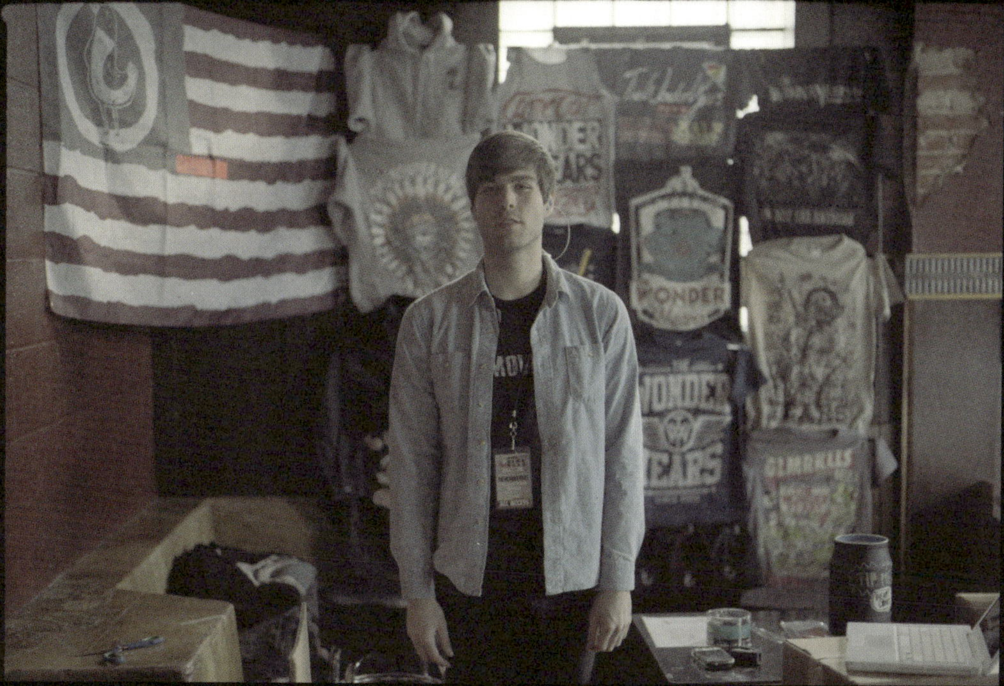
WONDER

GILDAN
SETTING THE STANDARD
www.gildan.com

GILDAN

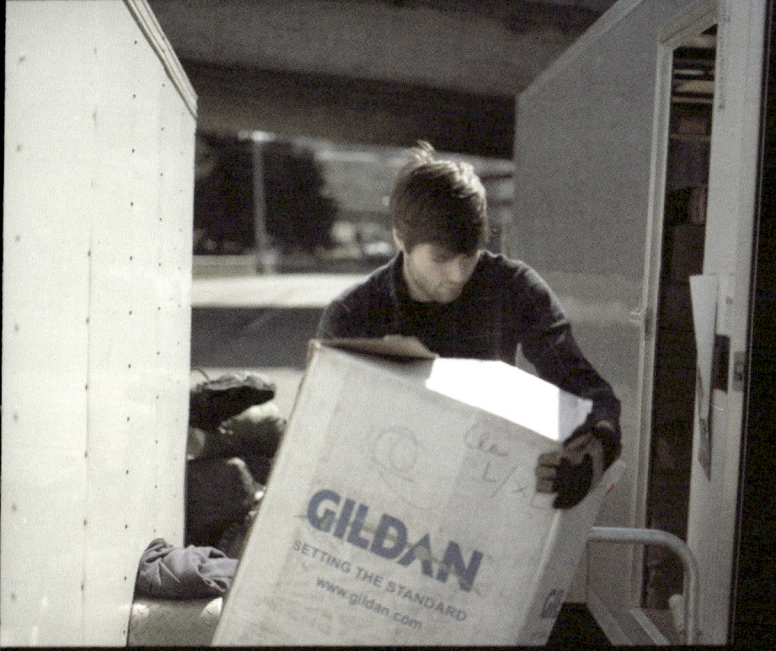

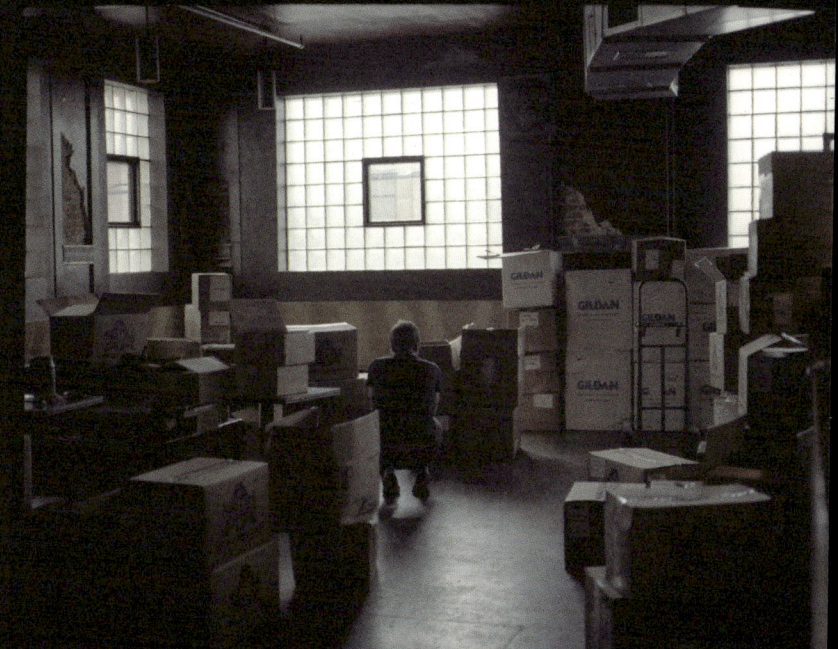

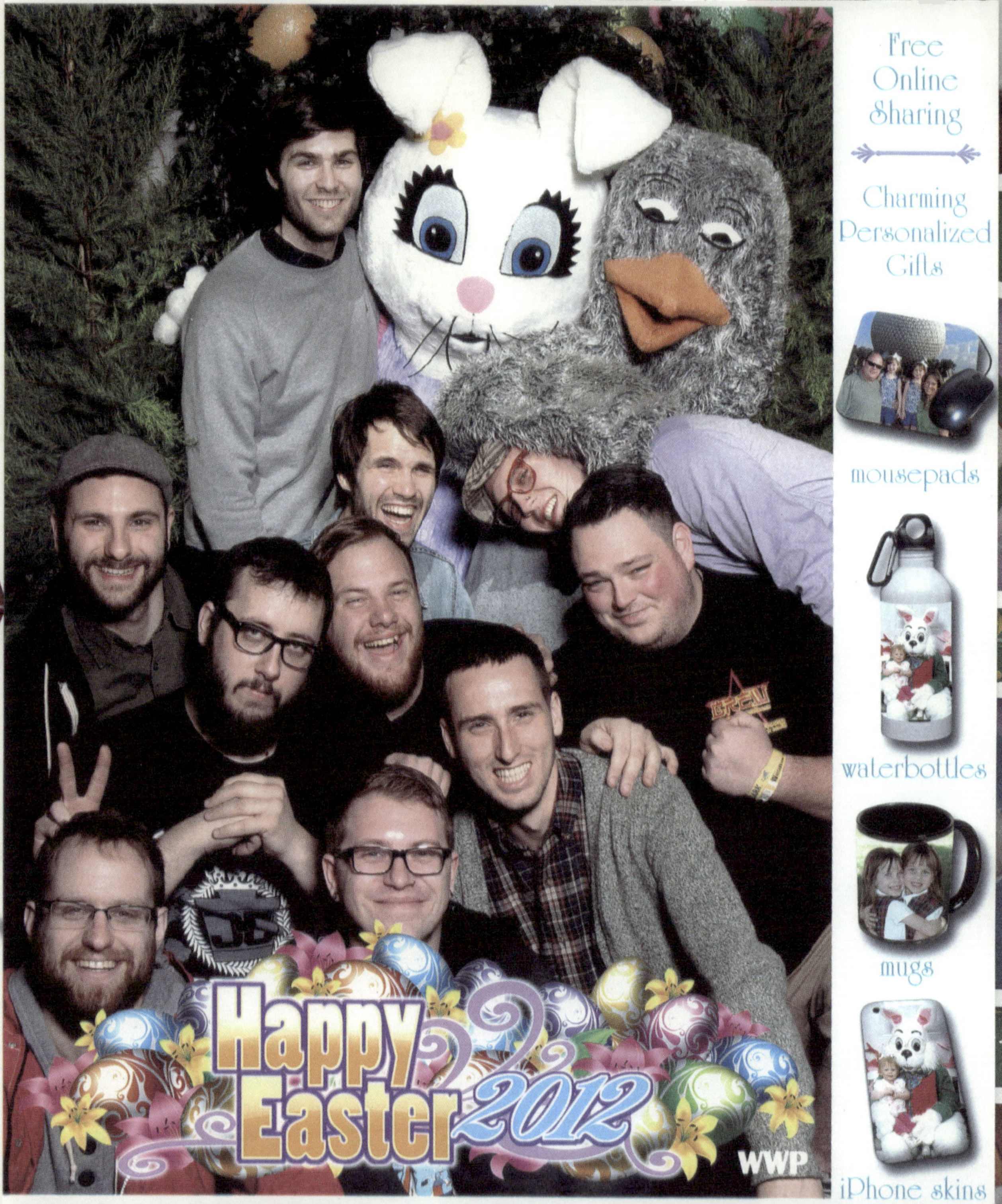

Free Online Sharing

Charming Personalized Gifts

mousepads

waterbottles

mugs

iPhone skins

Happy Easter 2012

Security circled us for 10 minutes, finally says something and then radios in to say he's "made contact with the duck."

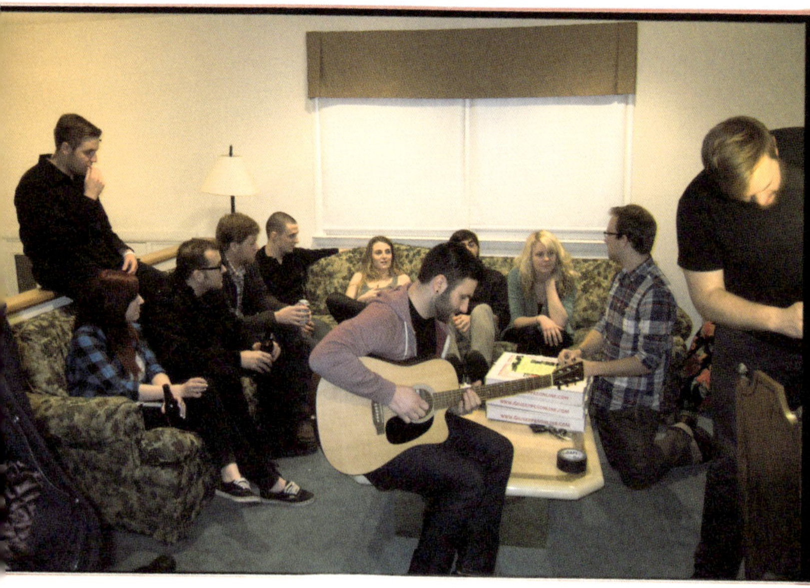

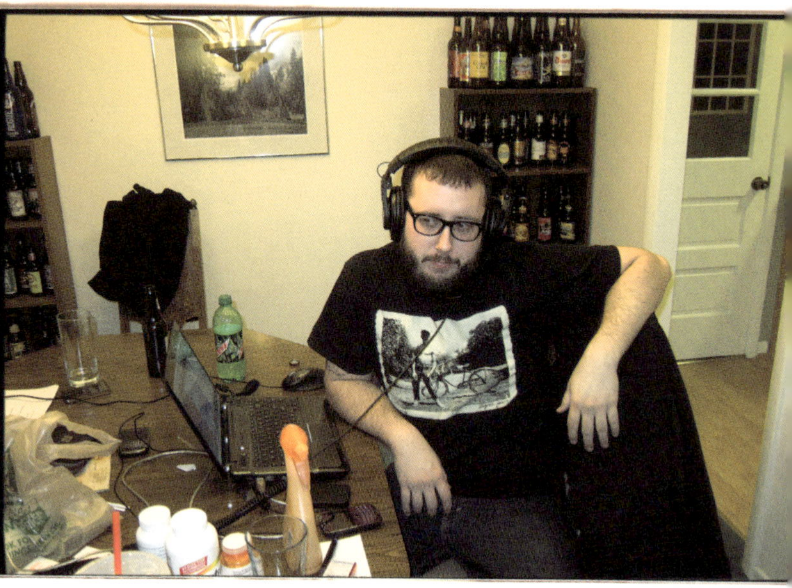

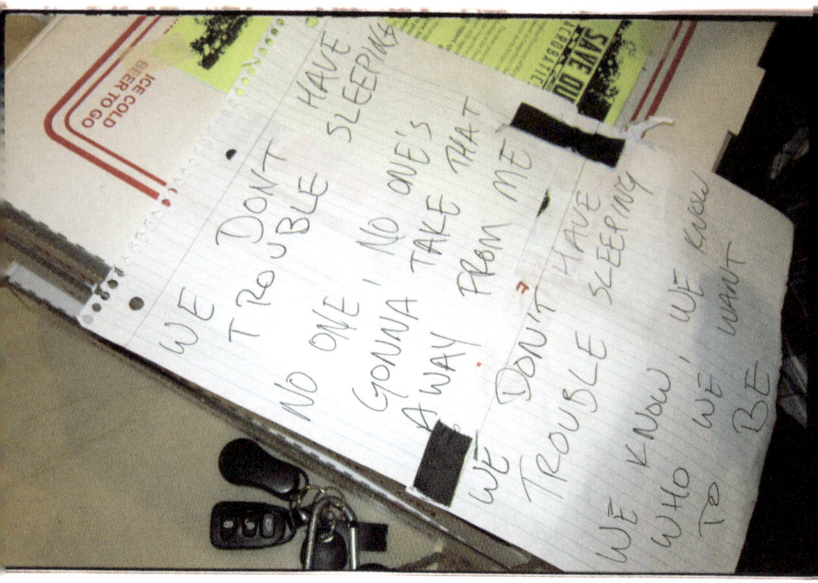

WE DON'T HAVE
TROUBLE SLEEPING
NO ONE, NO ONE'S
GONNA TAKE THAT
AWAY FROM ME
WE DON'T HAVE
TROUBLE SLEEPING
WE KNOW WE KNOW
WHO WE WANT
TO BE

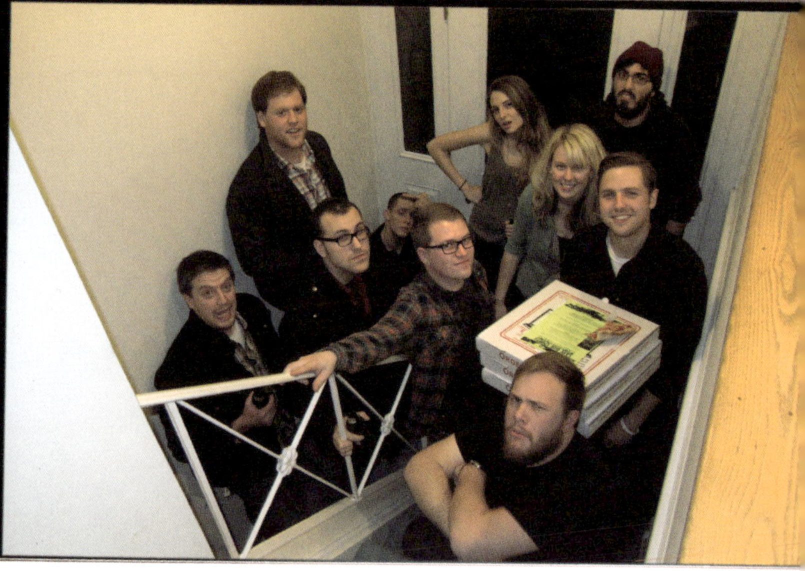

Chicago, IL. Two Shows. Sold Out. One Day. Bottom Lounge. 3/17/12

Bacon Maple Bar ✓ — Miami Vice ✓
Portland Cream ✓ — Double Bubble ✓
Capt. My Capt. ✓ — Apple Fritter ✓
Grape Ape ✓ — The Loop ✓
Mango Tango ✓ — Sprinkle ✓
Marshall Matters ✓
Memphis Mafia ✓
Old Dirty Bastards ✓
Arnold Palmer ✓
Raspberry Romeo ✓

I'm not totally sure if it's the ADHD, the coffee, or a weirder deep-seated psych issue, but I have a truly insatiable lust for travel, adventure, and more specifically, food. Lucky for me, some sort of cosmic alignment has allowed me and my friends a job that has taken us around the world more times than I can count.

I'm not super sure how we/I got here, but I'm sure as hell not going to waste it. There is only one thing I want out of life, just the humble desire to experience every single facet of everything life offers.

—MAK

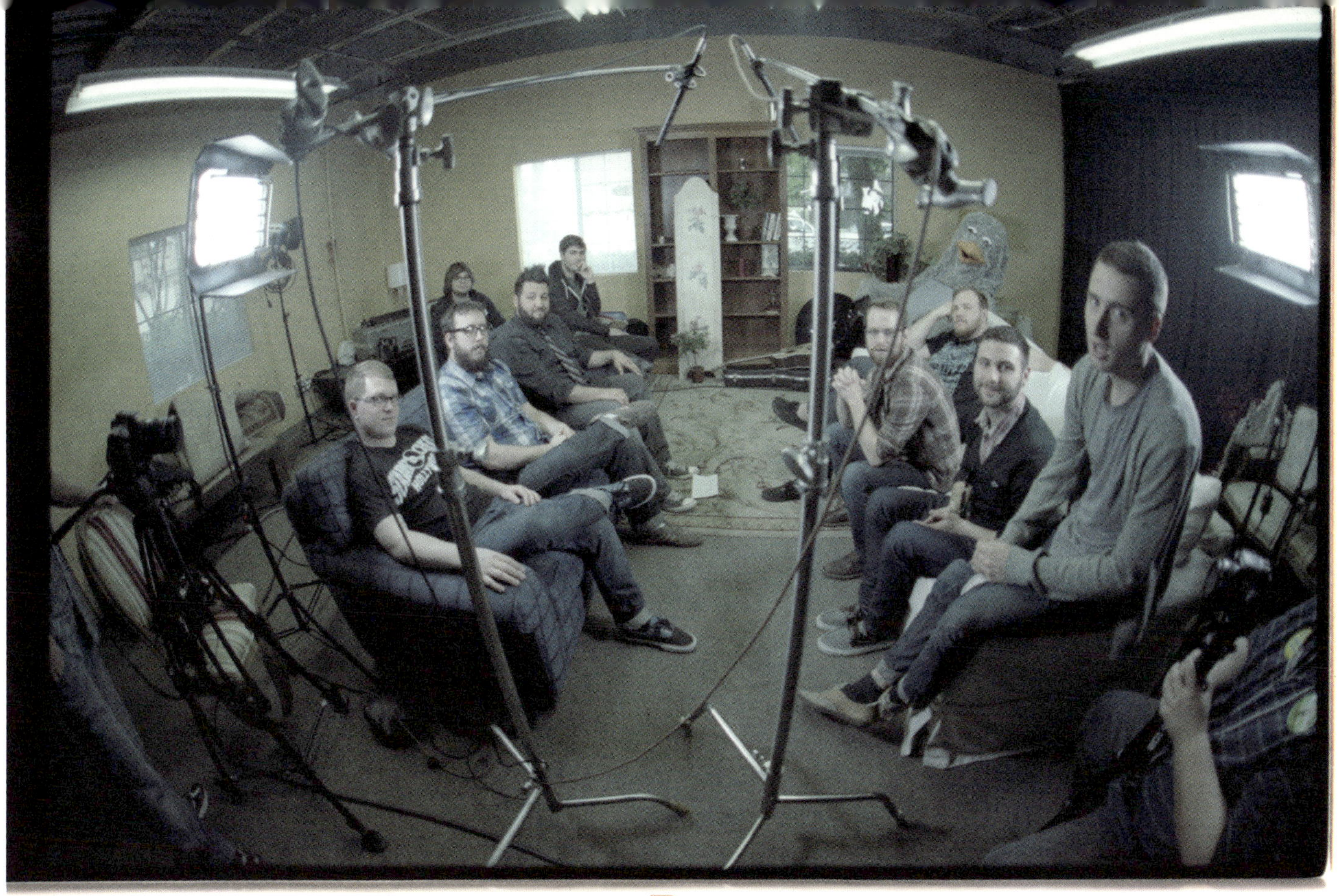

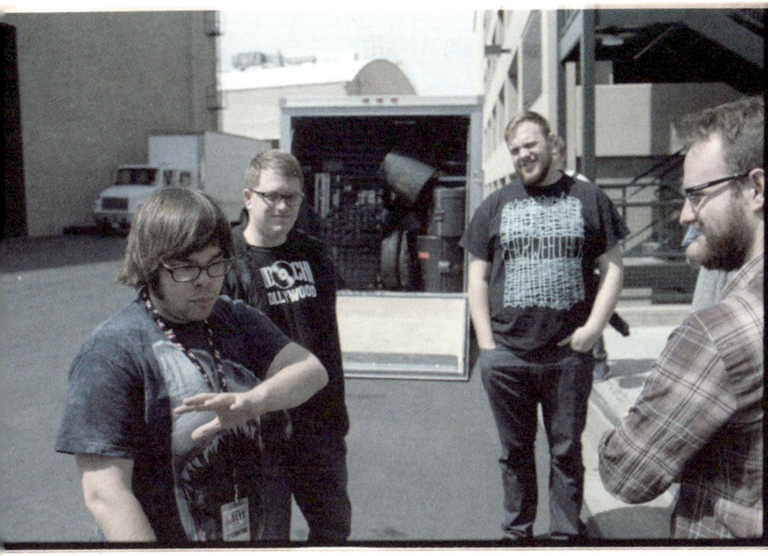

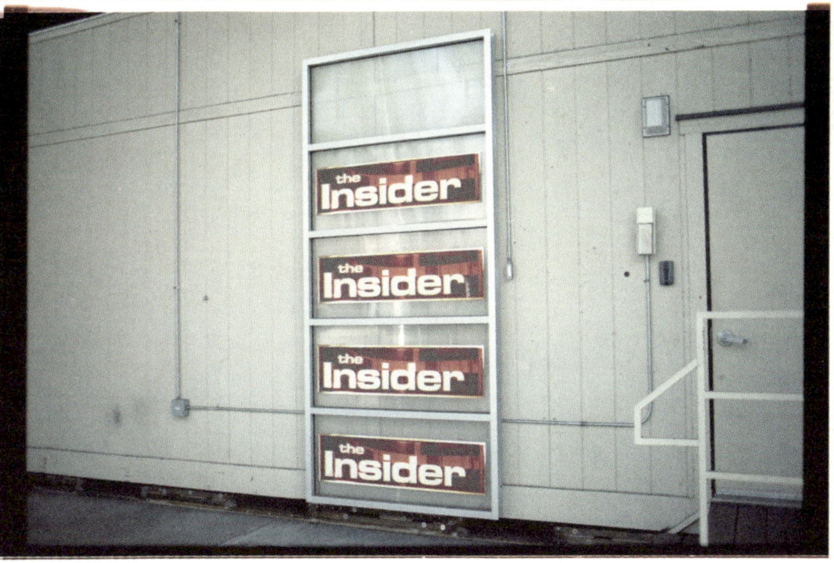
the Insider
the Insider
the Insider
the Insider

WAFFLE HOUSE

NO FRIENDS

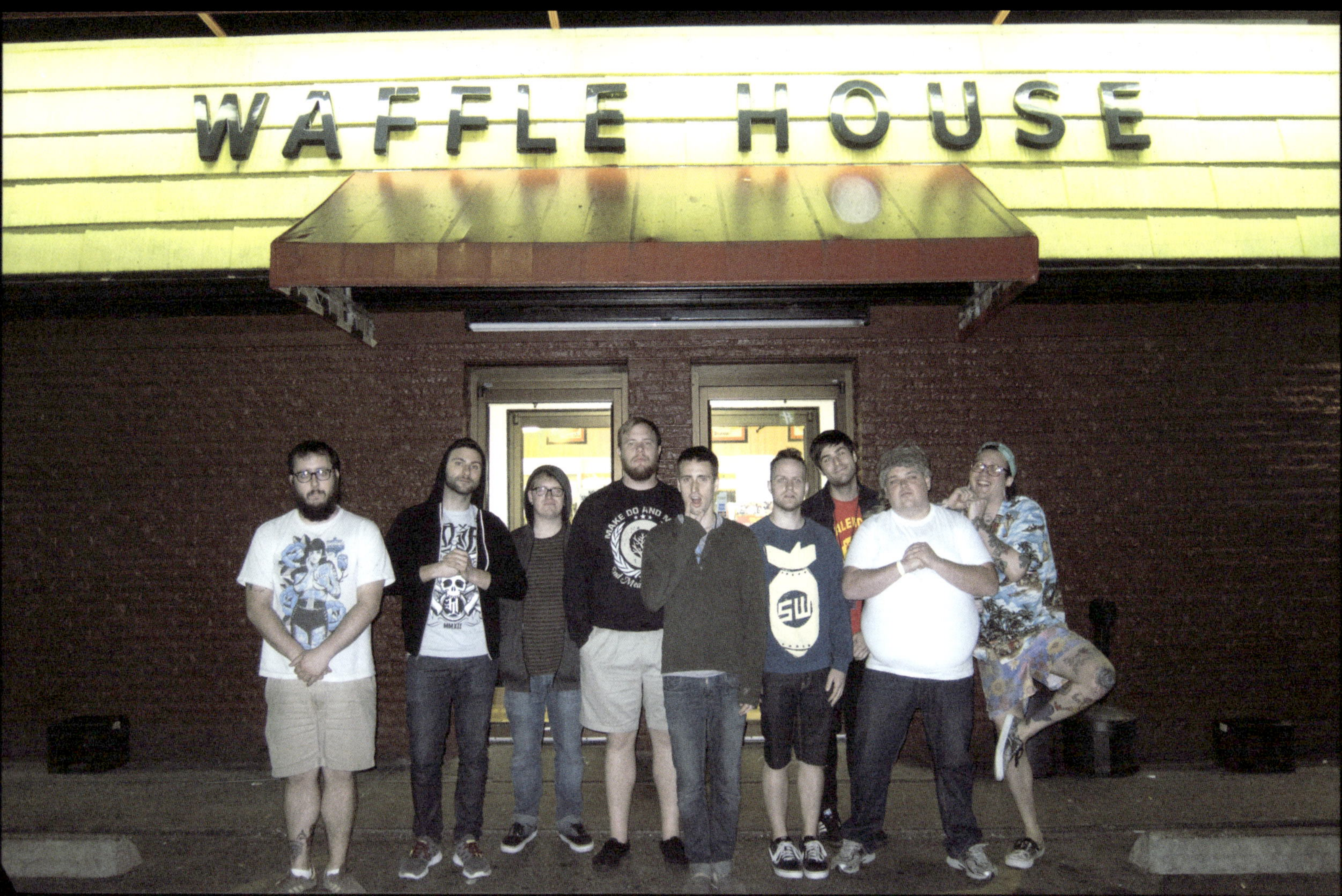

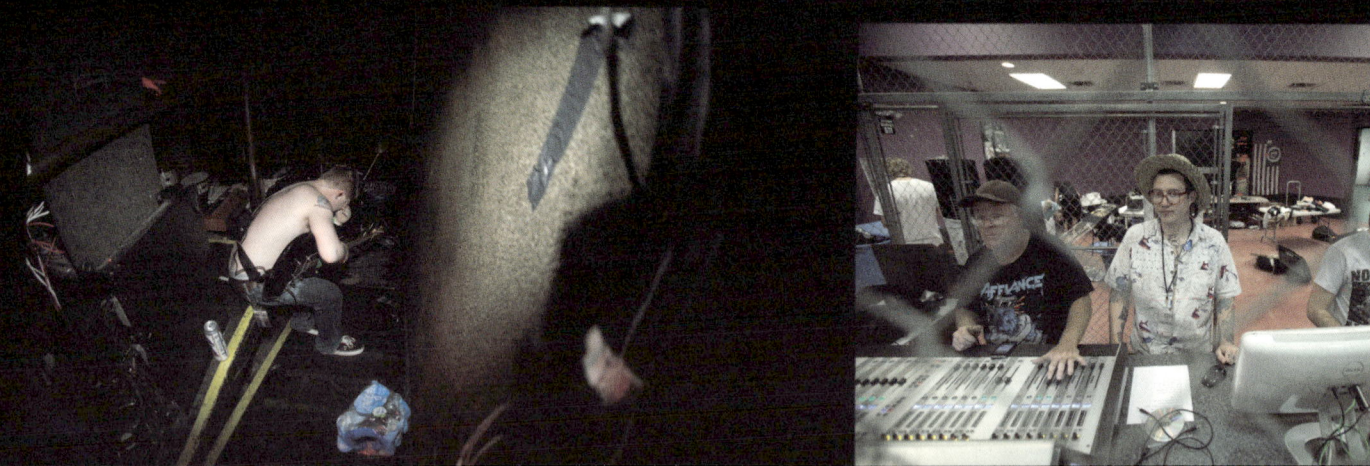

LOS ANGELES,

# CALIFORNIA

Mitch kept pushing to me that in Little Rock, there was an awesome second-hand shit store. He also told me he knew where it was. The second part was a lie. After wandering for a bit, we found it and legit had to push through a lobby filled with clutter to get in. Inside, part of the store was closed because a pile of items had a minor avalanche and wasn't safe to be near. Inside we found and bought a lot of awesome shit, including Simpsons bobble-heads and a life-sized Undertaker cut out. The other half of the store was a gay sex shop. The owner assumed Mitch and I were gay and informed us that, if he could watch, he would let us have sex in the shop. He also tried to sell us a beanie baby with a huge penis and followed us outside and down the block. Great day. -DC

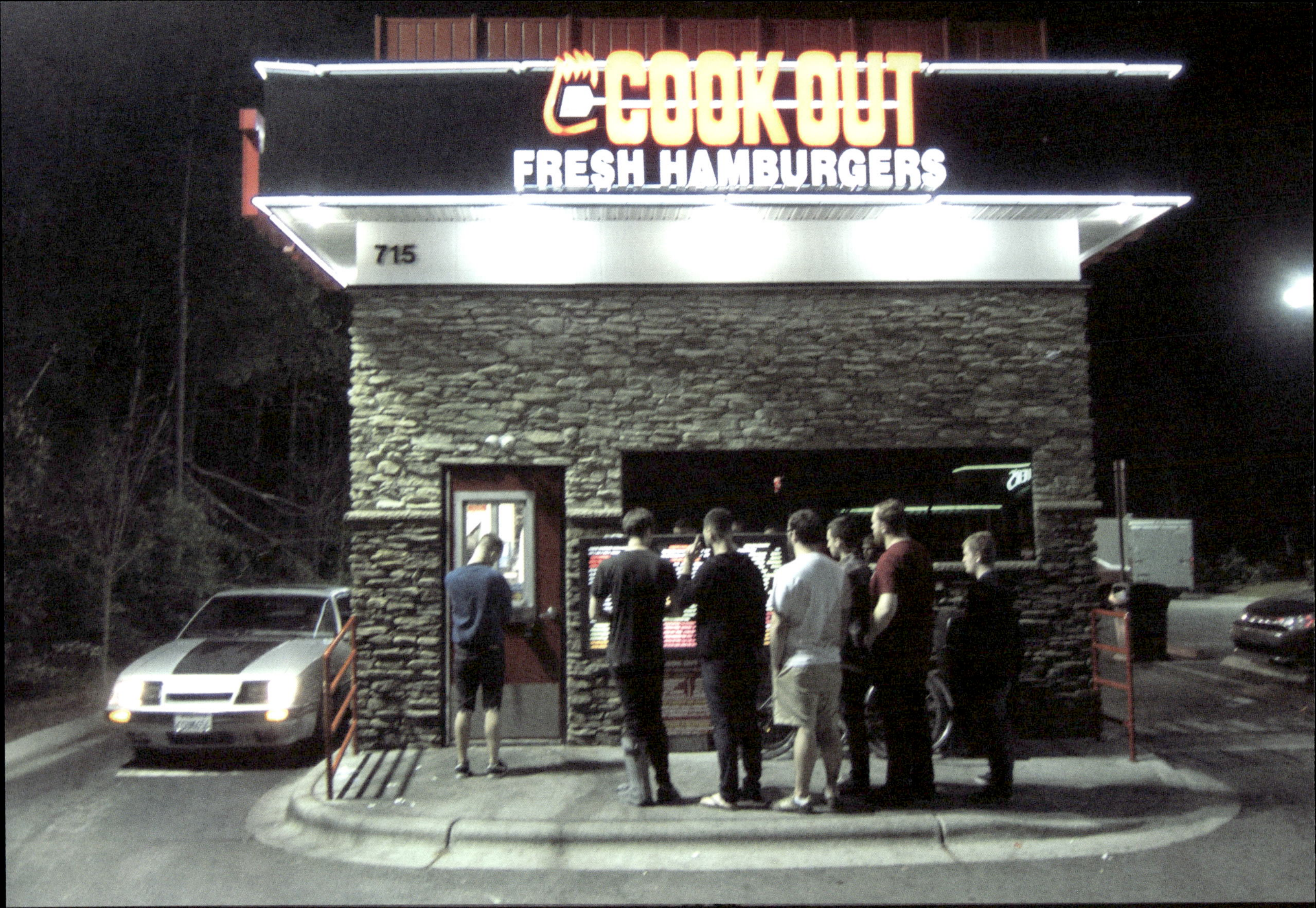
COOK OUT
FRESH HAMBURGERS
715

COOK OUT
"Cooked Outdoors Style!"®
Original Hamburgers
&
"Creamery"
36
Premium

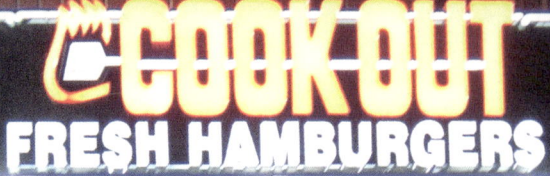

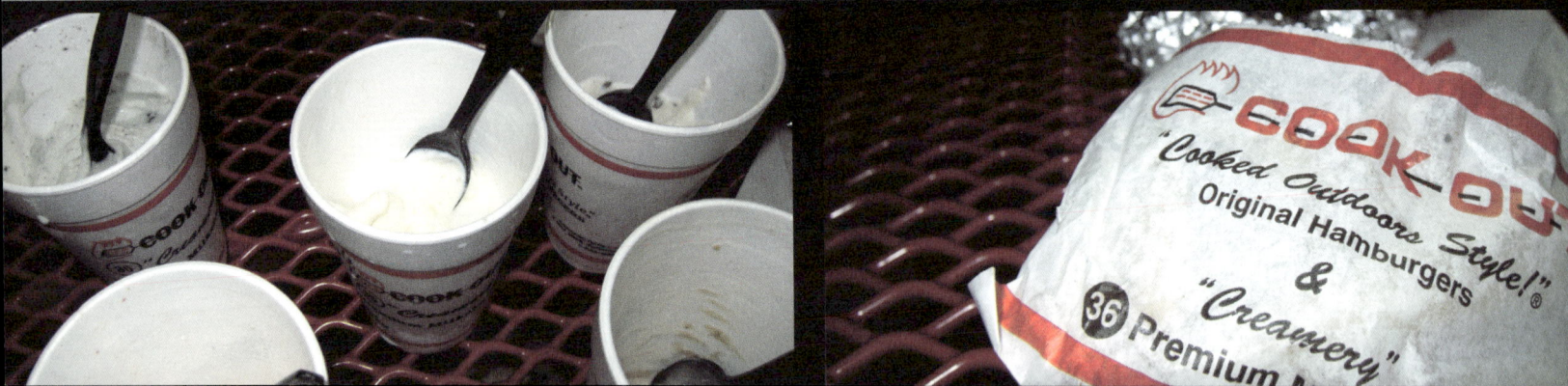

GOLDEN GATE BRIDGE, IT RAINED MOST OF THAT DAY BUT IT WAS KIND OF NICE. I HAD TWO DINNERS THAT NIGHT - MW

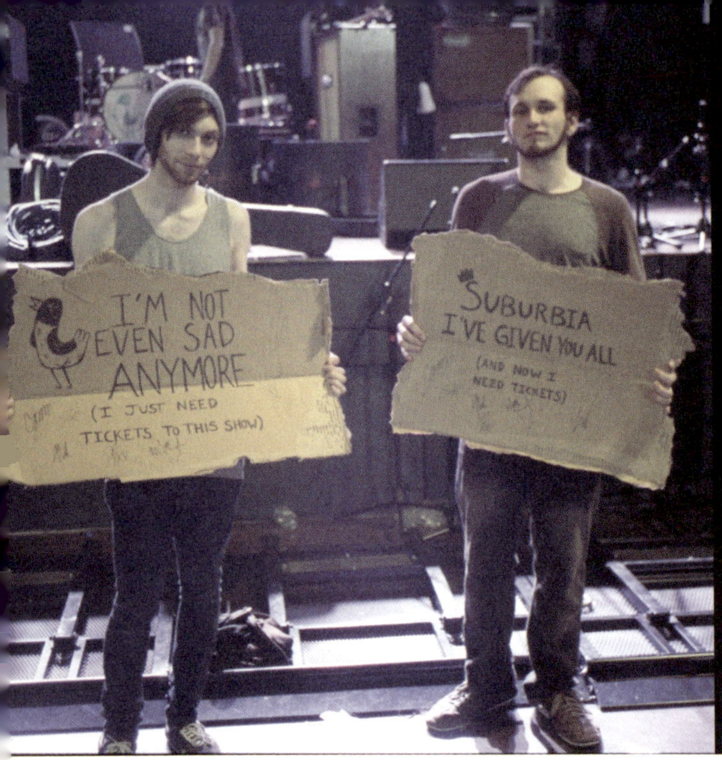
I'M NOT EVEN SAD ANYMORE
(I JUST NEED TICKETS TO THIS SHOW)
SUBURBIA I'VE GIVEN YOU ALL
(AND NOW I NEED TICKETS)

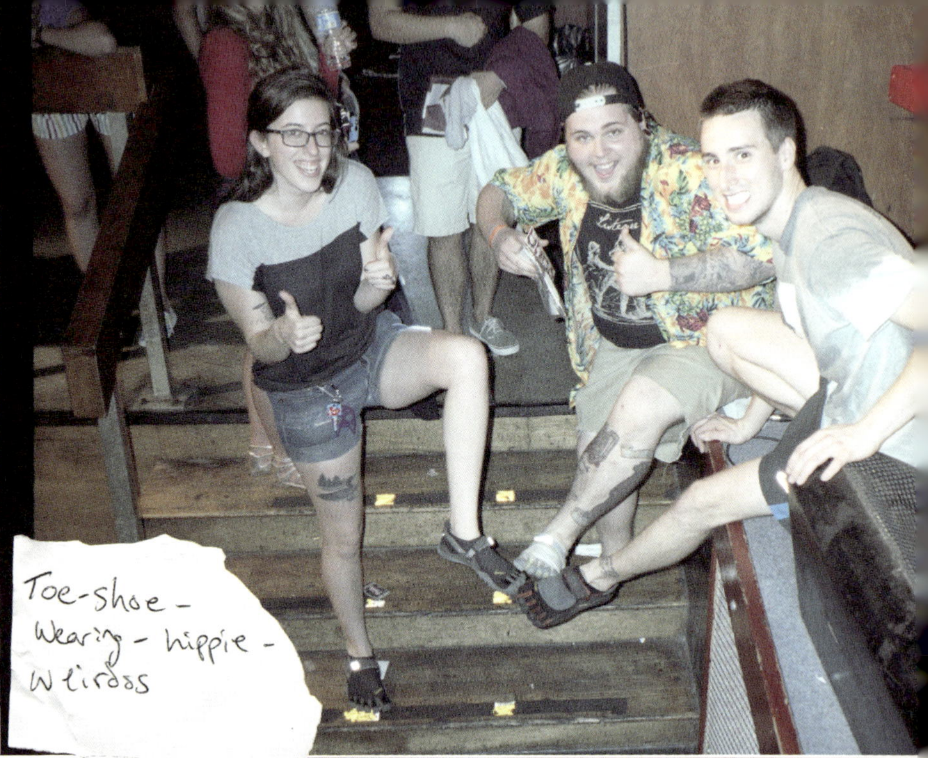

Toe-shoe-Wearing-hippie-Weirdos

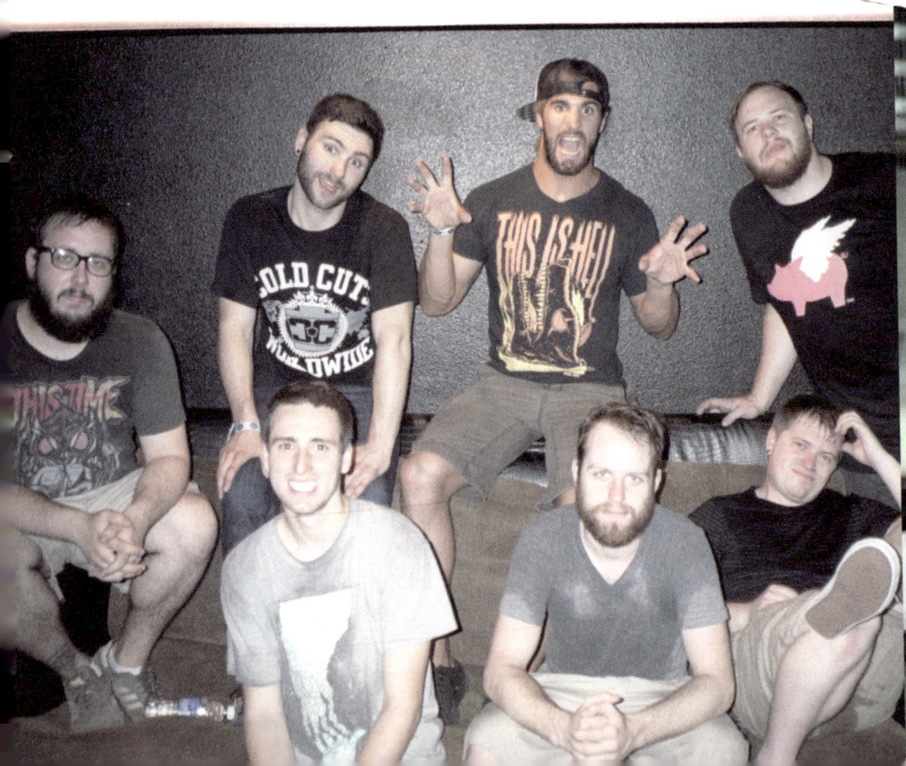
THIS IS HELL

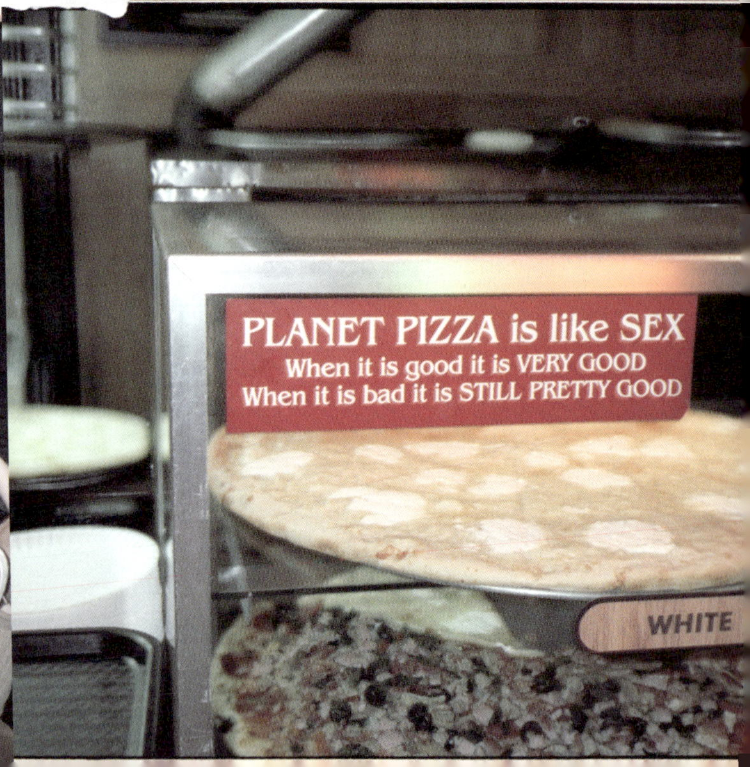
PLANET PIZZA is like SEX
When it is good it is VERY GOOD
When it is bad it is STILL PRETTY GOOD
WHITE

Someone told me that killing an Ybor City chicken was considered murder. I just wanted to catch one to have a van-chicken. I didn't succeed. I did succeed in eating a tenth of my body weight in our two trips to Taco Bus that day. Pineapple Water. Seriously.

— NS

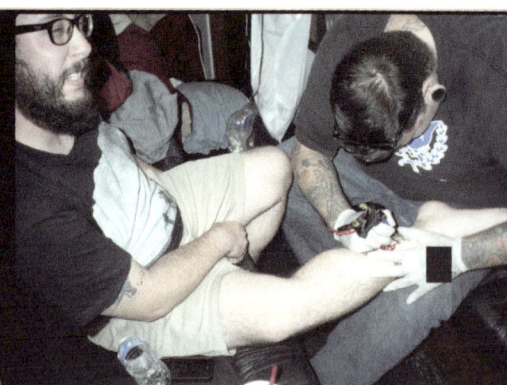

| Friday    March 16th, 2012 | Time Zone: Eastern |
|---|---|
| HAPPY 3:16 FUCKERS | Cleveland, OH |

| | | Venue Type: | Ages: | Capacity: |
|---|---|---|---|---|
| Venue: | Peabody's Down Under<br>2083 East 21st Street<br>Cleveland, OH 44115 | CLUB | ALL | 700 |
| | | Schedule: | LOAD IN: | 02:00:00 PM |
| Phone: | | TWY | SOUNDCHECK: | 3-415PM |
| Fax: | | TSSF/IIOI | SOUNDCHECK: | 430-540pm |
| | | | DOORS: | 06:00:00 PM |
| **PARKING NOTES & MISC.:** | | | INTO IT OVER IT: | 645-715PM |
| | | | THE STORY SO: | 730-8PM |
| Parking in street in front of the venue | | | TRANSIT: | 815-845PM |
| Load in through the front door. | | | PBC: | 9-940PM |
| | | | WONDER YEARS: | 10-1105PM |
| | | | CURFEW: | n/a |
| | | Meal: | Buyout: | Merch %: |
| | | n/a | YES | 90/10% |
| | | Stunners?: | Banner: | Barricade: |
| | | YES | hmm... | no |
| | | Dressing Room: | Shower: | Wi/Fi |
| | | 2 | NO WAY! | yes |
| P | | | | |
| Cell: | | Wireless = N/W: Peabodys no p/w | | |
| Email: | | | | |
| Production: | | | | |
| Cell: | | PRESS: | | |
| Email: | | – In person interview | | |
| Settle: | IF Sellout – early settle | Mandatory flipping of the bird all day cause | | |
| Loaders: | 2 | STONE COLD SAID SO. | | |
| Light board: | THREE SIXTEEN | | | |

| BUS CALL: | | Midnight | |
|---|---|---|---|
| Traveling to Chicago, IL CST | | | |
| MILES: | 350 | EST TIME: | 6 hours |
| After Show Notes! | | | |
| Tomorrow is another double show! OVERNIGHT DRIVE! EARLY LOAD INS! 830AM for TWY. 930-10AM everyone else. | | | |

Our dressing room in Houston
-MB

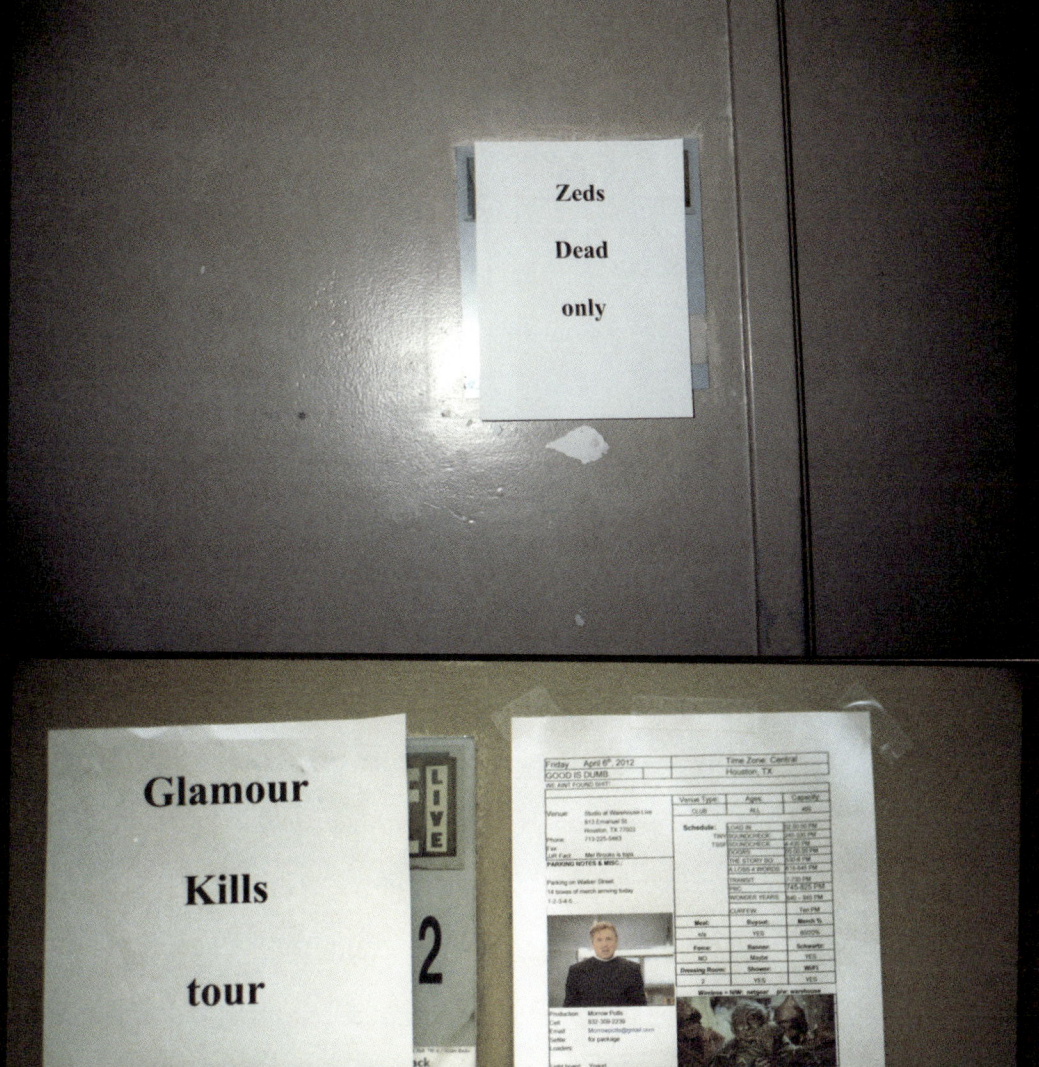

Sometimes after a hard days work you need a beer. Sometimes you need 7. —AM
Sometimes you find Matty in the street getting wild. Sometimes you go to a rave. Shit happens.

This is Mitchell's car. It is an incredible piece of shit. Fortunately for us it was in Orange County when we were recording "Suburbia..." and he let us use it all the time. Soupy and I actually got pulled over while driving it and the cops realized it was such a piece of shit that there is no way we could've stolen it. Great police work! Now I think this hunk of crap is for sale. Ask Chris from No Sleep Records about it.

-Am

Chris at the No Sleep office
— MB

Stormtracker turned out to be spot on.
—MB

This rest stop won an award back in 1992. - NS

Excellent USA paraphernalia at this middle-of-nowhere rest stop. We left them a Wonder Years Nation Flag. -DC

I was told to write something funny about our day in New York. Is "I slept sitting up on the couch" funny enough? Because that's what I did. All day.
   -NS

Superlatives... yup, just like in highschool. We had the greatest time on this tour with everyone, so like, why not? I would like to thank Cook Out for serving me five different milkshakes with my order, helping me win "fattest shitty" and making my parents proud. - MW

Credits:

Visual:
All photographs (with very few exceptions) taken by Mitchell Wojcik.
Additional photographs taken by Jamie Moore, Matt Brasch, Dan Campbell, Casey Cavaliere, Nick Steinborn and Josh Martin.
Layout by Mitchell Wojcik.
Additional art direction by Dan Campbell.
Hand Lettering for cover by James Heimer.

Cameras used for this book: Contax T2, Olympus Stylus, Leica Mini3, Mamiya AFD, Kiev 60, Fuji Instax, Polaroid Land Camera 420, a disposable camera from Walgreens and two others from Walmart, Canon EOS 1-N, Canon 5DmkII, Canon 5D, Canon 60D, Cannon T3i, Canon S95, some Lomo camera I found at a show, iPhone 3GS, iPhone 4, Blackberry Bold 9650, and a discontinued Samsung phone.

The Wonder Years Touring Party Included: Matt Brasch (guitar/vocals), Dan Campbell (vocals), Casey Cavaliere (guitar/vocals), Mike Kennedy (drums), Josh Martin (bass/vocals), Nick Steinborn (guitars/keys), John James Ryan Jr (tour manager/merch/stage right), Mitchell Wojcik (photographer/drum tech), Marc Langlois (merch), James Googe (Nintendo hype guy), Jenny Douglas (assistant tm/mustache tech), Jesse Barnes (bus driver), Tom Juba (DJ Tommy J), Luke Schwartz (fuck school tech), Justin Oscapinski (party tech), John Smith (English driver), Ryan Wapner (merch/lights), Conor O'Brien (driver/stage left) and "Young" Drew Magid (merch).

Audio:

Tracks 1-13 produced, engineered and mixed by Steve Evetts.
Tracks 14 and 15 engineered and mixed by Nick Steinborn.
Tracks 16-18 engineered and mixed by Eric Tuffendsam.
Track 19 recorded by Ryan Russell.
Tracks 20-24 recorded live in Nick and Kennedy's basements (see notes below).
Tracks 1-13 mastered by Alan Douches.
Tracks 14-24 mastered by Bill Henderson.

Tracks 20-21 - Don't Let Me Cave In and Came Out Swinging - 11.26.10 - These are the last demos of these songs that we recorded before actually heading west to record. Bass and drums were recorded together and a the guitars were recorded together. Vocals were done in a take or two just to get the idea down. These are the demos that I actually wrote my keyboard parts on.

Track 22 - Coffee Eyes - 11.14.10 - Coffee Eyes was one of the few songs that we had a minimal start on before getting together in the basement. This was recorded live only five days after we started writing. Everything g mic'd up quickly and we ran a line out from the PA for the vocals.

Track 23 - Woke Up Older - 11.18.10 - This was maybe the 4th time we played the song in its entirety. We trie to change up the intro because Dan insisted that it sounded too much like Pennywise. That didn't last. Sadly my rippin' solo didn't last either. This version was recorded live with two mics haphazardly placed in the roor

Track 24 - It's Murder Suicide - 11.29.10 - Sometimes you have days where you can't write anything. This wa our answer to writers' block. We played this riff for probably an hour and a half before "composing" this "song Sometimes you just gotta mosh it out.

-NS

The Wonder Years is Matt Brasch, Dan Campbell, Casey Cavaliere, Josh Martin, Mike Kennedy and Nick Steinborn.